W9-BYR-819

Hollywood's Most Wanted

Also by Floyd Conner

Hollywood's Most Wanted

The Top 10 Book of Lucky Breaks,
Prima Donnas, Box Office Bombs,
and Other Oddities

Floyd Conner

Brassey's, Inc.

WASHINGTON, D.C.

Copyright © 2002 by Brassey's, Inc.

Published in the United States by Brassey's, Inc. All rights
reserved. No part of this book may be reproduced in
any manner whatsoever without written permission from
the publisher, except in the case of brief quotations
embodied in critical articles and reviews.

Library of Congress Cataloging-in-Publication Data

Conner, Floyd, 1951–
  Hollywood's most wanted : the top 10 book of lucky
breaks, prima donnas, box office bombs, and other
oddities / Floyd Conner.
    p.   cm.
Includes bibliographical references and index.
  ISBN 1-57488-480-8 (pbk.)
  1. Motion pictures—Miscellanea. I. Title.
PN1998 .C54 2002
791.43—dc21

                              2002008006

Printed in Canada.

Brassey's, Inc.
22841 Quicksilver Drive
Dulles, Virginia 20166

Designed by Pen & Palette Unlimited.

First Edition

10 9 8 7 6 5 4 3 2 1

Contents

List of Photographs

Introduction

*H*ollywood's Most Wanted recognizes the movie industry's outstanding offenders. This book contains top 10 lists of the biggest flops, worst flubs, and most outrageous actors in movie history. The lists include the most outrageous gimmicks, unbelievable publicity stunts, biggest scandals, worst films, inauspicious film debuts, embarrassing Oscar moments, and intriguing urban legends.

Before they were stars, many actors had unusual jobs. Warren Beatty took a job as a rat catcher in a Washington, D.C., theater. Jack Nicholson's first job in Hollywood was answering fan mail at MGM for cartoon characters Tom and Jerry. Brad Pitt drove strippers to private parties. Sylvester Stallone cleaned out the lion cages at the Central Park Zoo. Al Pacino worked as a restroom attendant. Two-time Oscar winner Dustin Hoffman had jobs as a toy demonstrator and psychiatric attendant.

Not every actor was recognized immediately for his or her potential. An early evaluation of Fred Astaire concluded, "He can't act, can't sing, slightly bald, can dance a little." It was thought that Clark Gable looked like an ape and was too ugly to be a movie star. Conversely, Jerome "Curly"

Howard was originally considered too handsome and not funny enough to join the Three Stooges. Paul Newman was said to have no sex appeal. Louis B. Mayer took one look at Greta Garbo and told her she was too fat to be a star. Clint Eastwood was not considered star material because the studio thought his Adam's apple was too large.

Actors don't always make the right choice of their film roles. George Raft turned down both *The Maltese Falcon* and *Casablanca.* Humphrey Bogart accepted both films and became a superstar. James Caan passed on both *One Flew Over the Cuckoo's Nest* and *Kramer vs. Kramer,* but the roles won Oscars for Jack Nicholson and Dustin Hoffman. Norma Shearer rejected the lead in *Mrs. Miniver* because she didn't want to play a mother. Greer Garson stepped in and won a Best Actress Oscar. Brigitte Helm rejected the part of Lola Lola in *The Blue Angel,* and the role made Marlene Dietrich a film icon.

Movie stars have had some strange pets. John Barrymore owned a vulture named Mahoney. George Clooney had a pet potbellied pig. Best Actor Oscar winner Emil Jannings had a coop full of chickens, each named after a Hollywood star. When Ava Gardner died in 1990, her will instructed that her dog would have his own maid and chauffeur.

Former President Ronald Reagan wasn't the only actor who went into politics. George Murphy was elected to the U.S. Senate from California. Jesse Ventura, the ex-wrestler who starred in *Predator,* was elected governor of Minnesota. Actors Fred Grandy and Ben Jones both served in the U.S. House of Representatives. Child star Shirley Temple has served as U.S. representative to the United Nations, U.S. ambassador to Ghana and the former Czechoslovakia, and White House Chief of Protocol.

This book introduces nearly 700 of Hollywood's most wanted performers. Their offenses range from bad acting to outrageous behavior. Be on the lookout for them.

Opening Credits

*W**ings* was the first film to win an Academy Award for Best Picture. The following list features some other notable film firsts.

1. BLACK MARIA

The first movie studio opened in West Orange, New Jersey, on February 1, 1893. Known as Black Maria because of its black roofing paper, the studio was built as part of the Edison Laboratories. Inventor Thomas Edison made some of the earliest films at Black Maria. The building was constructed at a cost of $637 and featured an ingenious design that allowed it to revolve so it could always face the sun.

2. HOLLAND BROTHERS KINETOSCOPE PARLOR

The first commercial presentation of motion pictures occurred on April 14, 1894, at the Holland Brothers Kinetoscope Parlor. The parlor was located at 1155 Broadway, New York City. For a quarter, a person could watch five kinetoscopes from the Edison Studio. Some of the short movies available for viewing included a barber cutting hair, a blacksmith shoeing a horse, a wrestling match, a highland dance, and a cockfight. On its first day, the kinetoscope parlor had 500 customers.

3. ALICE GUY

The first woman film director was Alice Guy. In 1900, she directed a film, *La Fee au Choax,* shot at the Gaumont Studio in Paris. Guy later became head of the Gaumont Studio and helped launch the career of the acclaimed director Louis Feuillade.

4. THE STORY OF THE KELLY GANG

The first full-length motion picture, produced in Australia in 1906, told the story of the Kelly Gang and cost only $450 to make. The action film inspired directors such as D. W. Griffith and Cecil B. De Mille to make feature films in the United States.

5. ASTA NIELSEN

The first film superstar was a German actress named Asta Nielsen. She was paid $53 for her film debut in *The Abyss* in 1910; two years later she earned $80,000. By contrast, the highest-paid stars in the United States earned less than a fifth of what Nielsen was paid in Europe. Nielsen's stardom was brief, and she later became the manager of a cinema in Copenhagen.

6. EUGENIE BESSEMER

The first woman to have a speaking role in a motion picture was Eugenie Bessemer: she spoke 13 words in the first talking picture, *The Jazz Singer*, in 1927. The film, which starred Al Jolson, had several musical numbers, but most of it was silent.

7. NORMA TALMADGE

The tradition of movie stars leaving their footprints in cement at Grauman's Chinese Theater began by accident. In 1927, silent film actress Norma Talmadge stepped in wet cement, giving theater owner Sid Grauman the notion of asking stars to leave their footprints in cement in front of the cinema. Thanks to the gimmick, Grauman's Chinese Theater became one of Hollywood's biggest tourist attractions.

8. *LIGHTS OF NEW YORK*

The first all-talking motion picture was Warner Brothers' *Lights of New York*, released in 1928. The film's success proved that *The Jazz Singer* was no fluke. Within a year, virtually all Hollywood films were talkies.

9. ACADEMY AWARDS

The first Academy Awards ceremony was held in the Blossom Room of the Hollywood Roosevelt Hotel on May 16, 1929. The evening was more a banquet than an awards presentation. Three hundred guests dined on squab Perigeaux, lobster Eugenie, and terrapin. Janet Gaynor was the first Best Actress winner, and Emil Jannings won the Best Actor award. There was no suspense, however; the winners had been announced three months earlier. The first televised Academy Awards ceremony was not until 1953.

10. **CAMDEN AUTOMOBILE THEATER**

The first drive-in was the Camden Automobile Theater in New Jersey, which opened on June 6, 1933. The first feature film was *Wife Beware* starring Adolph Menjou, and admission was 25 cents per person.

Odd Jobs

Before they were movie stars, many would-be actors worked menial jobs. Some of their odd jobs really were odd. Oscar winner Geena Davis was employed as a human mannequin in a New York women's clothing store window. Another Oscar winner, David Niven, worked as an indoor pony-racing promoter. Bruce Willis claimed he was a bigger star as a New York City bartender than he is as a movie star. Comedian Jerry Lewis was fired an hour after he began work as a soda jerk when he forgot to take the peel off the banana in a banana split. Debonair Cary Grant earned a living as a sandwich man on stilts. Bob Hope was a professional boxer who fought under the name of Packy West. One of James Dean's earliest jobs was as a stunt tester on the television game show, *Beat the Clock*. Imagine having the glamorous Sharon Stone waiting on you at McDonald's. Both Elvis Presley and Barbra Streisand worked as movie ushers before making the leap to the silver screen. Woody Harrelson claimed he was fired from 17 jobs in one year.

1. **WARREN BEATTY**

When he was 17 years old, Warren Beatty hung around the National Theater in Washington, D.C., in the hopes of being hired. Beatty was given a job, but not what he was expecting. The aspiring actor was hired as a rat catcher. Rats were entering the theater from a backstreet alley and biting the actors. Beatty was stationed in the alley during a revival of Thornton Wilder's *The Skin of Our Teeth* starring Helen Hayes.

After moving to New York City, Beatty worked a series of odd jobs. Beatty toiled as a sandhog in the Lincoln Tunnel and he played piano on an early morning religious program. His breakthrough into acting came as an accident. A friend asked him to go on an audition and help him read for a part. Beatty got the part instead. Since that time, Beatty has starred in such films as *Bonnie and Clyde, McCabe and Mrs. Miller,* and *Shampoo.*

2. **JACK NICHOLSON**

Three-time Oscar winner Jack Nicholson is considered Hollywood's consummate actor. He began his show business career sorting fan mail for the cartoon characters, *Tom and Jerry,* at the MGM studio. The actor, who now earns millions of dollars per picture, earned $30 a week.

Nicholson joined an acting repertory group known as The Players Ring that included young actors Michael Landon, Edd Byrnes, and Robert Fuller. A talent scout attended a performance of *Tea and Sympathy* and signed Landon, Byrnes, and Fuller to contracts while Nicholson was ignored. As a result, Landon was cast as Little Joe in *Bonanza,* Byrnes got the role of Kookie in *77 Sunset Strip,* and Fuller starred as Jess

Harper in *Laramie.* When Nicholson finally had his first screen test, he froze and forgot all his lines. For more than a decade he appeared in low-budget horror and biker films before his breakthrough in *Easy Rider* in 1969.

3. **SYLVESTER STALLONE**

A sickly child, Sylvester Stallone was nicknamed Sylvester the Cat because he had a slight speech defect. His dramatic debut was as Smokey the Bear in a Cub Scout play; Stallone suffered the indignity of playing the lower half of the bear. In school, he tried out for a part in a play, but he was so bad he vowed never to act again. He was earning $38 a week as a movie usher when he was fired for charging patrons $5 extra to seat them sooner. Hired as an attendant in the Central Park Zoo, the Italian Stallion quit after a lion urinated on him. Stallone became an action superstar in the *Rocky* and *Rambo* movies.

4. **AL PACINO**

Before he became a successful actor, Al Pacino worked a variety of jobs, including as a furniture mover and an usher in an East Side New York movie theater. For a year he cleaned toilets as a $14-a-week building superintendent. Pacino later earned a reputation as one of the movies' greatest actors in films such as in *The Godfather, Scarface, Dog Day Afternoon,* and *Scent of a Woman.*

5. **DUSTIN HOFFMAN**

Dustin Hoffman made his dramatic debut as Tiny Tim in a seventh-grade production of *A Christmas Carol.* He was chosen for the role because he was the shortest student at John Burroughs High School. Hoffman was suspended when he said, "God bless us, everyone, goddammit."

Hoffman worked as a hat checker in The Longacres Theater in New York, was a janitor in a dance studio, and weaved Hawaiian leis. For three Christmases he worked in the toy department at Macy's. Perhaps his oddest job was as a psychiatric attendant in a mental hospital.

Once he turned to acting, it took five auditions before Hoffman was finally accepted into the Actors Studio. In his Broadway debut, he had a one-word walk-on role as a soldier in the flop, *A Cook for Mr. General.* Hoffman became a star on Broadway playing a hunchbacked German homosexual in the play, *Harry, Noon, and Night.* In 1967, Hoffman rose to film stardom in *The Graduate.*

6. **BRAD PITT**

Superhunk Brad Pitt once worked as a chauffeur for Strip-O-Gram. Pitt drove strippers to nightclubs and private parties to deliver their messages. Another job Pitt would rather forget was dressing up as the chicken mascot for El Pollo Loco Restaurant. Pitt became one of the most popular stars of the 1990s in films such as *Thelma and Louise* and *Twelve Monkeys.*

7. **GRETA GARBO**

Greta Garbo was the most glamorous of all movie stars. Before she came to Hollywood, Garbo was paid a dollar a week to lather men's faces in a Swedish barber shop. From the time she arrived in Hollywood in the mid 1920s, to her retirement in 1942, Greta Garbo was one of Hollywood's greatest stars.

Brad Pitt in *Seven Years in Tibet* (1997).

8. CHARLIE CHAPLIN

As a youth in London, Charlie Chaplin earned 60 cents a week as a janitor. Two years after he arrived in Hollywood, Chaplin was earning $10,000 per week. He went on to direct and star in such comic masterpieces as *The Gold Rush, The Circus, City Lights,* and *Modern Times.*

9. ALAN LADD

Alan Ladd worked at a Piggly Wiggly store as a teenager. He was turned down at the Universal Studio Acting School because they thought he was too short to be an actor, so Ladd opened a hot dog stand outside the studio gates to get noticed. The plan did not work, but Ladd began getting small roles in films during the 1930s. In 1942, Ladd became a star in his role as a hit man in *This Gun for Hire.*

10. **STEVE McQUEEN**

Steve McQueen held many different jobs before he became an actor. He was a ballpoint pen salesman, a carnival huckster, a lumberjack, and an errand boy in a brothel. While working as a television repairman in Greenwich Village, he met several actors who encouraged him to try acting. McQueen later starred in film hits such as *The Great Escape* and *Bullitt.*

Big Breaks

I n 1927, when director Mervyn LeRoy called actress Polly Ann Young to see if she was interested in his next film, *Naughty but Nice,* Polly's 15-year-old sister, Loretta, answered the phone. Loretta Young got the role instead and launched a long and successful film career, highlighted by a Best Actress Oscar in 1947. Here's how other movie stars got their big breaks.

1. RONALD REAGAN

After college, Ronald Reagan was hired as a radio announcer for station WHO in Des Moines, Iowa. Reagan announced the Chicago Cubs baseball games, and every March he visited California, where the Cubs played their spring training games. Reagan was introduced to agent Bill Meiklejohn, who arranged a screen test at Warner Brothers. The studio was looking for an actor with an all-American quality to portray a radio announcer in the movie, *Love in the Air.* The actor originally cast in the role, Ross Alexander, had committed suicide. Reagan was signed to a seven-year contract starting at $200 per week, and his acting career lasted more than 25 years.

2. **MEL GIBSON**

Mel Gibson got into a fight on the eve of his audition for the action film, *Mad Max,* and arrived at the audition with a black eye. Director George Miller hired Gibson partly because of his roughed-up appearance, which was perfectly suited to the character Mad Max. The film became an international hit, and made Gibson a major movie star.

3. **MARLENE DIETRICH**

Glamorous star Marlene Dietrich originally wanted to be a concert violinist, but her dreams were shattered when she pulled a ligament in her middle finger while playing a Bach sonata. She was reduced to playing background music at a theater during silent movies.

By chance, Dietrich was invited to the castle of celebrated producer Max Reinhardt, where she entertained the guests by playing a musical saw. As she played the saw, Dietrich spread her gorgeous legs. Reinhardt took notice and signed Dietrich to a contract. In 1929, Dietrich created a sensation with her role as Lola Lola in *The Blue Angel.*

4. **JOHN WAYNE**

Marion Morrison was a prop man at Fox for three years before his big break occurred. The 6-foot, 4-inch former football player was unloading a truckload of furniture when he was noticed by director Raoul Walsh. Walsh arranged for a screen test, and Morrison was signed to a $75-a-week contract and cast in the director's next film, *The Big Trail.* The studio decided to change Morrison's name to John Wayne, and a star was born.

5. **CLARK GABLE**

Clark Gable was working as a telephone repairman when he was called to fix the telephone of drama coach, Josephine Dillon. She fell in love with Gable, who was 14 years younger than she, and they married. Dillon gave him acting lessons and, under her guidance, Gable became one of Hollywood's most popular leading men. In 1934, he won a Best Actor Oscar for his performance in *It Happened One Night.*

6. **LANA TURNER**

According to legend, Lana Turner was discovered while sipping a soda at Schwab's Drug Store. In fact, Turner was discovered at Tops on Sunset Boulevard by Billy Wilkerson, publisher of *The Hollywood Reporter.* He took the attractive teenager to the Zeppo Marx Agency. The agency had trouble getting Turner a contract however, and a casting director at 20th Century-Fox angrily told her agent not to waste their time with an actress with so little talent. Eventually, Turner landed a contract at Warner Brothers and rose to stardom during the 1940s.

7. **SHIRLEY MACLAINE**

The show business term, "break a leg" had a different meaning for Shirley MacLaine. In May 1954, MacLaine was an understudy for actress Carol Haney in *The Pajama Game* on Broadway. When Haney broke her ankle, MacLaine inherited the lead role. Two nights later, she was spotted by producer Hal Wallis, who arranged for her to have a screen test. MacLaine was signed to a seven-year contract and quickly became a star.

8. **MARILYN MONROE**

In 1946, Howard Hughes was recuperating from injuries suffered in an airplane crash. While he was in the hospital, he saw a sexy blonde on the cover of a popular men's magazine of the day, *Laff.* The producer had helped launch the film careers of Jean Harlow and Jane Russell, and he believed his new find would be his latest sex symbol discovery. Word of Hughes's interest leaked out, and the young actress signed a contract with 20th Century-Fox. They changed her name to Marilyn Monroe, and she became the greatest sex symbol in film history.

9. **ROCK HUDSON**

Roy Scherer was delivering the mail when he was noticed by superagent Henry Willson. Willson brought the handsome mailman to the attention of director Raoul Walsh, who cast him in his film, *Fighter Squadron,* in 1948. After a name change, Rock Hudson became one of the biggest stars of the 1950s.

10. **TOM SELLECK**

Tom Selleck appeared as a contestant on *The Dating Game.* The game show featured a bachelorette who asked questions of three bachelors who were sitting behind a screen. Selleck was so nervous that he froze and was not selected for the date. Given a second chance, Selleck was rejected once again, but he did catch the eye of a talent scout from Universal Studio who arranged a screen test. Eventually, Selleck signed with 20th Century-Fox. Hardly an overnight success, Selleck appeared in the critically panned *Myra Breckenridge* and as a corpse in *Coma.* He made six unsuccessful television pilots before success finally came, in *Magnum, P.I.*

Inauspicious Debuts

F ew stars begin at the top. Harrison Ford's first film appearance consisted of one line as a bellboy in the 1966 movie,
Dead Heat on a Merry-Go-Round. From this inauspicious beginning, Ford later starred in movie blockbusters such as *American Graffiti, Star Wars,* and *Raiders of the Lost Ark.* Many stars
have launched their screen careers in bit parts or low-budget
films.

1. ARNOLD SCHWARZENEGGER

Arnold Schwarzenegger won seven Mr. Olympia and five Mr.
Universe bodybuilding titles. His first film, *Hercules in New
York,* gave him plenty of opportunities to show off his mag-
nificent physique. The 1969 film featured Schwarzenegger
as Hercules in modern-day New York. In a dreadful scene,
Schwarzenegger fought with a man in a grizzly bear suit.
Arnold's English was so bad he had to be dubbed. Unde-
terred by his initial failure as an actor, Schwarzenegger finally
achieved success with the title role in 1982 in *Conan the
Barbarian.*

2. MARILYN MONROE

Few would have guessed that Marilyn Monroe was going to become a star from her first film role. Her debut was in the 1948 film, *Scudda Hoo! Scudda Hay!,* a barnyard drama about a farmer and his team of mules. Monroe's role consisted of a walk-on, and her only line was, "Hi." The scene ended up on the cutting-room floor. Two years later, Monroe was finally noticed in a supporting role in the Oscar-winning drama, *All About Eve.*

3. JAMES DEAN

Many believe that James Dean only appeared in three films. He is remembered for his starring roles in *Rebel Without a Cause, East of Eden,* and *Giant.* Actually, Dean had appeared in several films before playing those roles. His first film was a 1951 Jerry Lewis and Dean Martin comedy, called *Sailor Beware.* Dean played a boxing cornerman and was on camera for less than a minute. His only line: "That guy's a professional."

4. JACK NICHOLSON

Jack Nicholson's first featured role was in the low-budget film *Cry Baby Killer,* in 1958. The film, produced by Roger Corman, cost only $7,000 to make, and, in it, Nicholson played a juvenile delinquent who shoots two men. Before he became a star in the early 1970s, Nicholson appeared in several Roger Corman films, most memorably as a masochistic dental patient in *Little Shop of Horrors* (1960).

5. KEVIN COSTNER

Kevin Costner would like to be remembered for his roles in blockbuster films such as *Dances with Wolves* and *Field of*

Dreams. Costner's first screen appearance, however, was in a 1976 turkey, called *Sizzle Beach U.S.A.* Costner's rise to stardom was slow. In 1983, he played the corpse at the beginning of *The Big Chill,* in a role so small they didn't even show his face.

6. BILLY CRYSTAL

In Billy Crystal's film debut, *Rabbit Test* (1977), he played the world's first pregnant man. *Rabbit Test* was so bad it has been called one of the worst films ever made. Crystal rebounded with hits such as *When Harry Met Sally* and *City Slickers.*

7. CLINT EASTWOOD

Clint Eastwood's first film role was as a lab technician in the 1955 horror movie *Revenge of the Creature,* the sequel to *The Creature from the Black Lagoon.* Eastwood was a regular on the television western *Rawhide,* before reaching stardom in the 1964 spaghetti western *A Fistful of Dollars.*

8. MICHAEL LANDON

Like Jack Nicholson, Michael Landon got his first starring role in a Roger Corman film playing the title role in *I Was a Teenage Werewolf* (1957). Landon never did become a major film star, but on television, it was a different story. Landon starred in the tremendously popular *Bonanza* and *Little House on the Prairie* series.

9. SYLVESTER STALLONE

Most actors would love to have their motion picture debut in a Woody Allen film. Sylvester Stallone's first screen role was as a mugger on a New York subway in Allen's 1970 comedy, *Bananas.* It would be another five years until Stallone hit the big time with his role as a boxing underdog in *Rocky.*

10. **RICHARD DREYFUSS**

The Graduate (1967) was the film that made Dustin Hoffman a star. It also marked the film debut of Richard Dreyfuss, who had a brief role as a college student. By the mid-1970s, Dreyfus had starred in the megahits, *Close Encounters of the Third Kind* and *Jaws*.

A Star Isn't Born

S tar potential is not always evident. Jane Russell failed her first screen test because she was considered "too unphotogenic." Cary Grant failed his first screen test at Paramount because studio executives thought his neck was too thick. It was said of Spencer Tracy that he was, "too ugly to be a leading man, but not ugly enough to be a villain." After Sophia Loren's failed first screen test, she was told that her hips were too big and her nose too long for her to become a star. Director D. W. Griffith told a young Mary Pickford that she was too little and too fat to be in the movies. As a contestant on *Ted Mack's Amateur Hour,* Ann-Margret lost to a performer who played "Lady of Spain" on a leaf. Elvis Presley's eighth-grade teacher told him he had no promise as a singer. Tom Cruise was voted the Least Likely to Succeed in high school. Richard Dreyfuss flunked out of drama school.

1. FRED ASTAIRE

In 1933, Fred Astaire was given his first screen test. Already an international dancing sensation, Astaire did not impress studio executives. One observed, "He can't act, can't sing, slightly bald, can dance a little." Astaire proved his detractors wrong by becoming one of the top box office draws of the 1930s in films such as *Top Hat* and *Swing Time.*

2. GRETA GARBO

One of the most glamorous of all stars, Greta Garbo was not deemed star material originally. She began her film career in her native Sweden. MGM studio head Louis B. Mayer had brought Garbo's mentor, director Mauritz Stiller, to America, and Garbo accompanied Stiller to New York. Mayer took one look at Garbo and told her, "We don't like fat girls in this country." Garbo's arrival was so ignored that she had to pay a photographer $10 to take her photo. Stiller convinced Mayer to sign Garbo to a contract, however, and she became a film legend.

3. BETTE DAVIS

No one could have guessed from her screen tests that Bette Davis would have one of the longest and most successful acting careers in Hollywood history. After seeing her first test, Davis ran screaming from the screening room. Universal Studio head Carl Laemmle said, "She has as much sex appeal as Slim Summerville." When director Michael Curtiz was looking for an attractive actress to play a Southern belle in *Cabin in the Cotton* (1932), someone suggested Davis. "Are you kidding?" Curtiz replied, "Who would want to go to bed with her?"

4. CLARK GABLE

Clark Gable suffered the indignity of several failed screen tests. When he arrived in Hollywood in 1930, Gable had rotten teeth and had not yet grown his signature moustache. Irving Thalberg, MGM production chief, on seeing Gable's test exclaimed, "It's awful, take it away!" Noting Gable's large ears, producer Howard Hughes said, "He looks like a taxicab with both doors open." Jack Warner chastised his assistant for even giving Gable a screen test, asking, "Why did you throw away $500 of our money on a test for that big ape?" Gable was so discouraged he almost left Hollywood.

5. ELIZABETH TAYLOR

Elizabeth Taylor's acting career was almost over before it even began. When she was nine, a casting director complained that her violet eyes were "too old" for her to be a successful child actress. He proclaimed, "This kid has nothing."

6. GENE HACKMAN

As a young actor, Gene Hackman enrolled in The Pasadena Playhouse. Voted the least likely to succeed in the group, Hackman was not invited back the next season. He proved them wrong, however, by winning two Academy Awards and becoming one of Hollywood's most respected actors.

7. WOODY ALLEN

Woody Allen has been an award-winning actor, screenwriter, and director, but the comic genius dropped out of New York University in 1953 after failing a film production course. He broke into show business by selling jokes for 10 cents each to such unlikely comedians as bandleader Guy Lombardo, dancer Arthur Murray, columnist Earl Wilson, and television host Ed Sullivan. Allen was so nervous on his opening night as a stand-up comedian at the Duplex Club in Greenwich Village he had to be pushed out on stage, and his act bombed so badly that he wasn't paid. He debuted as an actor in a supporting role in *What's New Pussycat?* starring

Peter Sellers. When he returned to filmmaking, he was so unsure of himself that he initially asked Jerry Lewis to direct his first film, *Take the Money and Run.*

8. CURLY HOWARD

Jerome "Curly" Howard was the most popular of the Three Stooges. The original Stooges were Moe Howard, Larry Fine, and Shemp Howard, but, when Shemp quit the Stooges to pursue a solo career, he recommended his younger brother, Jerry, as his replacement. At the time Jerome made his living as a ballroom dancer and sported long curly blonde locks. Initially, Ted Healy, who used the Stooges in his act, thought Jerome was not funny and was too handsome to be a stooge. Only after Shemp suggested Jerome shave his head did Healy agree to let him join the Stooges. The Stooges eventually left Healy and became one of the most popular comedy acts of all time.

9. ROCK HUDSON

Rock Hudson's screen test at 20th Century-Fox was so abysmal that it was shown to aspiring actors as an example of how not to act. Despite his horrendous screen test, Hudson became one of the most popular leading men of the 1950s and starred in such hits as *Giant* and *Written on the Wind.*

10. RUDOLPH VALENTINO

The first time director D. W. Griffith saw Rudolph Valentino, he said, "I don't think the girls will like him because he's too foreign-looking." Griffith could not have been more wrong: American women swooned over Valentino, who became the silver screen's first heartthrob.

Movie Moguls

The movie moguls of Hollywood's Golden Age were the most powerful people in Hollywood. These men could make or break a career.

1. SAM GOLDWYN

Born in Poland, Sam Gelbfisz (later Goldfish) was a glove salesman before getting into motion pictures. With Jesse Lasky and Cecil B. De Mille, he formed a studio that eventually became known as Paramount. Next, he teamed with the Selwyn brothers to form a company that evolved into Metro-Goldwyn-Mayer, and he changed his name to Goldwyn. Goldwyn's finest work came as an independent producer. His films include *The Best Years of Our Lives, The Pride of the Yankees, Dodsworth,* and *Ball of Fire.*

Goldwyn was known for mangling the English language, and his "Goldwynisms" have become a part of Hollywood lore. It was Goldwyn who said, "A verbal contract isn't worth the paper it's written on," and "Anyone who goes to see a psychiatrist ought to have his head examined." Goldwyn said he did not want yes men: "I want everybody to tell the truth—even if it costs them their jobs." When told one of his proposed pictures was too caustic, Goldwyn replied, "To hell with the cost, we'll make the picture anyway." He also said, "I don't care if my pictures don't make a dime, as long as everyone comes to see them."

Goldwyn always had helpful suggestions to his directors. He told one perplexed director, "Let's bring it up to date with some snappy nineteenth-century dialogue." To another he suggested, "What we want is a story that starts with an earthquake and works its way up to a climax." Another great idea by Goldwyn was, "I want to make a picture about the Russian secret police—the GOP."

Goldwyn boasted, "Our comedies are not to be laughed at," and said of another film, "It's more than magnificent—it's mediocre." He asked someone who had just seen one of his films: "Tell me, how did you love the picture?" He urged the public to see *Hans Christian Andersen* because it was "full of charmth and warmth."

Every successful man has a good woman behind him, as Goldwyn admitted, saying his wife was, "The best man I know." When he learned that Jesse Lasky was naming his son Bill, Goldwyn said, "Every Tom, Dick, and Harry is named Bill." Some of his most famous sayings showed his incredible leadership and decision-making abilities, including: "The next time I send a damn fool, I'll go myself," "I'll give you a definite maybe," "I don't make predictions about the future," "I can answer you in two words, im possible!" and "Include me out!"

Goldwyn was amazed when he saw a sundial at a Hollywood party: "Marvelous, what will they think of next?" Always keeping things in perspective, he remarked, "We have all passed a lot of water since then." When asked to write his autobiography Goldwyn shook his head and said, "Oh, no, I can't do that until long after I'm dead."

2. **HARRY COHN**

Harry Cohn ruled Columbia Pictures with an iron hand. Classic films made during Cohn's tenure included *It Happened One Night, The Awful Truth, Holiday, His Girl Friday, Gilda, The Lady from Shanghai, All the King's Men, From Here to Eternity, On the Waterfront,* and *The Bridge on the River Kwai.* Cohn said, "Screw the critics, I'm king here." His office was a replica of the office of one of his heroes, Benito Mussolini, and a secret passageway was built to it to accommodate his romantic trysts with young starlets.

Cohn claimed his ass itched when a film went on too long. After reading a one-page synopsis of *The Iliad,* he cleverly observed, "There are an awful lot of Greeks in it." Cohn told an aide he wanted a speech that everyone in the audience would recognize. When the man suggested Hamlet's soliloquy, Cohn said, "No, no, I mean something like, 'To be or not to be.'" His evaluation of Kim Novak: "She's got talent and personality. Give me two years and I'll make her an overnight star."

Cohn bragged, "I don't get ulcers, I give them." He installed an electric chair in the studio commissary to give a shock to unsuspecting employees. He once informed actor Farley Granger that he had won his services in a gin game the night before. Cohn said to Peter Falk, who had an artificial eye, "For the same money I could get an actor with two eyes." He referred to Marilyn Monroe as a "fat cow," and Hedda Hopper said of him, "You had to stand in line to hate him." Producer Sam Bischoff had it written into his contract that he would never have to speak to Harry Cohn. When Cohn died in 1958, Red Skelton joked about the huge turnout at his funeral: "It just goes to show you. Give the people what they want, they'll all show up."

3. **JACK WARNER**

During his tenure as head of production at Warner Brothers, Warner oversaw the making of great films, including *42nd Street, The Adventures of Robin Hood, The Maltese Falcon, Casablanca, Strangers on a Train, The Searchers,* and *Bonnie and Clyde.* Warner had his own unique way of determining how good a film was during a screening: the more times he got up to urinate, the less he liked it. His motto was, "Uneasy lies the head that wears the toilet seat." When Warner was introduced to Albert Einstein, he was informed that Einstein had invented the theory of relativity. Warner snapped back, "Well, professor, I have a theory of relatives, too. Don't hire them."

Warner did not want to make *Johnny Belinda,* which starred Jane Wyman as a deaf-mute, saying, "Who the hell wants to see a movie where the leading lady doesn't say a word?" The film was nominated for 12 Academy Awards, and Wyman won the Oscar for Best Actress.

When Warner Brothers threatened to sue the Marx Brothers for using *Casablanca* in the title of their 1946 comedy, *A Night in Casablanca,* Groucho wired Jack Warner: "And I'll sue you for using Brothers." Warner was upset when former Warner Brothers' contract player Ronald Reagan was elected governor of California: "It's our fault. We should have given him better parts." He thought Jimmy Stewart would make a better governor, and Ronald Reagan would be better cast as his best friend.

4. **DARRYL F. ZANUCK**

Darryl F. Zanuck worked his way up to become studio chief at 20th Century-Fox. *The Grapes of Wrath, How Green Was My Valley, Gentleman's Agreement,* and *All About Eve* were films made with Zanuck at the helm. Zanuck's intrusive meddling in the films made him unpopular with both actors and directors. Director Jean Renoir was so disgusted by Zanuck's changes to his 1941 film *Swamp Water* that he told the studio head, "It's certainly been a pleasure working for 16th Century-Fox." Zanuck felt the score for the 1936 film, *Under Two Flags*, was not French enough, so he suggested more French horns be added.

Zanuck's womanizing was legendary. He told an unimpressed Joan Collins, "You've had nothing until you've had me. I am the biggest and the best. I can go all night." His office was closed every afternoon at 4 o'clock so he could entertain young women.

5. **HOWARD HUGHES**

Howard Hughes produced his first film at age 19 and won his first Oscar at 21. As an independent producer, he made films such as *Hell's Angels, Scarface,* and *The Outlaw.* He presided over RKO Studios from 1947 to 1955, but it was rumored that Hughes never set foot on the RKO lot in all the years he owned the studio; reportedly he bought the studio to impress Ingrid Bergman. At one time Hughes had 108 starlets under contract, few of whom ever became stars. When Jimmy "the Greek" Snyder heard that Hughes had deflowered 200 virgins in Hollywood, he replied, "He must have got them all."

6. **LOUIS B. MAYER**

Louis B. Mayer said that there were more stars at MGM than there were in heaven. While production chief of MGM, Mayer made some of the most entertaining films in the history of cinema and raised the movie musical to an art form. Born in Russia, Mayer worked in the junk business before going to Hollywood. He liked to give the impression that everyone under contract to MGM was part of a big family. For example, he said of Wallace Beery, "Yes, Beery's a son of a bitch. But he's our son of a bitch." Robert Taylor, one of the studio's biggest stars, asked Mayer for a raise. Mayer put his arm around Taylor and said he was like a son to him. Taylor said later that he didn't get the raise, but he did gain a father.

Mayer was less popular with rival studio heads. Jack Warner said of him, "They say Louis B. Mayer was his own worst enemy. Not while I'm around." Mayer died in 1957, and his funeral was well attended. Sam Goldwyn explained, "The reason so many people turned up at his funeral is that they wanted to make sure he was dead."

7. CARL LAEMMLE

Carl Laemmle, president of Universal Studios, was known as Uncle Carl; he had a more kindly demeanor than most of the other moguls. During Laemmle's years at Universal, films produced included *The Phantom of the Opera, All Quiet on the Western Front, Frankenstein, Dracula, The Good Fairy,* and *My Man Godfrey.* In 1922, Laemmle was so alarmed when the budget of Erich von Stroheim's *Foolish Wives* kept going up that he had a giant electric sign erected on Broadway in New York City to kept track of the spiraling cost of the film. Once a week, a fire brigade would race to the sign to update the total.

8. ADOLPH ZUKOR

Adolph Zukor was born in Hungary and came to America with $40 sewn into his coat. Zukor, who lived to be 103 years old, was president of Paramount Studios. Marlene Dietrich, Gary Cooper, Bob Hope, Bing Crosby, Claudette

Colbert, and the Marx Brothers were a few of Paramount's stars during the Zukor years. In 1923, Zukor questioned Cecil B. De Mille about the lengthy shooting schedule for *The Ten Commandments.* De Mille replied, "What do you want me to do, stop shooting and release it as *The Five Commandments?*"

9. **DAVID O. SELZNICK**

David O. Selznick was an independent producer best known for making *Gone With the Wind.* Selznick's other credits include *A Star Is Born, Nothing Sacred, Rebecca,* and *Duel in the Sun.* Married to actress Jennifer Jones, Selznick was known to give lavish gifts to actresses. Joan Fontaine realized she was no longer a favorite of Selznick's when he sent her a $5 geranium for Christmas.

10. **HAL WALLIS**

Hal Wallis, a powerful and successful producer at Warner Brothers from 1933 to 1948, learned the hard way not to cross Jack Warner. When Wallis announced that he was leaving to take a job at Paramount, Jack Warner locked him out of his office. Undeterred, Wallis moved his desk to the studio lawn. Warner, wanting to have the last word, dumped a truckload of manure next to his desk.

Contract Players

A ctors sometimes have unusual stipulations written into their contracts. Silent film comedian Buster Keaton, known as "The Great Stone Face," was not permitted to smile in public. According to her contract, actress Lois Moran was not allowed to become more sophisticated for at least a year following the 1926 release of her film, *Stella Dallas*. Comedian Joe E. Brown was forbidden to grow a moustache. Joan Crawford's MGM contract in the early 1930s specified what time she had to go to bed at night. Silent film ingénue Mary Miles Minter was prohibited from getting married for at least three and a half years after signing her 1919 contract. Paramount threatened to void the contract of Frenchman Maurice Chevalier if he ever lost his accent.

1. JACK NICHOLSON

Jack Nicholson became a star with memorable performances in *Easy Rider* and *Five Easy Pieces*. When his friend, Henry Jaglom, directed his first film, *A Safe Place*, in 1971, Nicholson agreed to waive his large fee to appear in the movie: he agreed to star in the film in exchange for a color

Photofest

Jack Nicholson in *Easy Rider* (1969).

television. Years later, Nicholson was paid $50 million for his role as The Joker in *Batman.*

2. **THEDA BARA**

Theda Bara was the screen's first vamp. Although she was from Cincinnati, the studio wanted her to maintain the mysterious allure of Bara's exotic screen personas. She signed a contract with Fox in 1916 that had the following provisions:

1. She could not marry within three years.
2. She must be heavily veiled in public.
3. She could not appear in a theater.
4. She could not attend Turkish baths.
5. She could not pose for photographs.
6. She had to have the curtains of her limousine drawn at all times.
7. She could only go out at night.

3. **H. B. WARNER**

Director Cecil B. De Mille took his Biblical epics very seriously. He selected H. B. Warner for the coveted role of Jesus Christ in his 1926 film *King of Kings,* and, according to the contract, Warner could not accept any role during the next five years without De Mille's consent. In addition, Warner was prohibited from participating in any activity that might be considered offensive to Christians: he was barred from playing cards, going to nightclubs, riding in a convertible, and attending baseball games.

4. **SHIRLEY TEMPLE**

Child star Shirley Temple had a clause in her contract that demanded she have 56 curls in her hair. Lloyd's Of London inserted a clause into the contract of the seven-year-old actress that her insurance policy would be voided if she were ever killed or injured while drunk. Needless to say, the insurance company never had to exercise that option.

5. SYLVESTER STALLONE

Sylvester Stallone received 25 T-shirts for his first starring role, in *The Lords of Flatbush* (1974). Sixteen years later, Stallone was the highest-paid actor in Hollywood: he was paid $27 million plus 35 percent of the gross for *Rocky V.*

6. ELIZABETH TAYLOR

When Elizabeth Taylor was paid $1 million to play the title role in *Cleopatra* (1963), her contract specified that her husband, Eddie Fisher, would be paid $1,500 per day if he made sure she arrived on the set on time. Taylor was on time; however, she began a romance with Richard Burton that resulted in her divorcing Fisher.

7. MARILYN MONROE

Marilyn Monroe was underpaid during most of her movie career. Her salary, as stated in her 1953 contract with 20th Century-Fox, was $750 per month. That year she starred in the box office hits, *Gentlemen Prefer Blondes* and *How to Marry a Millionaire.* By comparison, Monroe's acting coach, Natasha Lytess, was paid $1,000 a month.

8. CAROLE LOMBARD

Carole Lombard was notorious for her practical jokes. When her agent, Myron Selznick (David O. Selznick's brother), gave her a contract to sign, she secretly changed the wording to read that she was entitled to 10 percent of Selznick's salary, the reverse of their normal agreement. Months later, Selznick was shocked when Lombard demanded a share of his earnings.

9. **BEN HECHT**

Ben Hecht signed a $5,000-a-week contract to coauthor (with Charles MacArthur) the screenplay for *The Unholy Garden* (1931) starring Ronald Colman. Hecht had a clause written into his contract that if meddlesome studio executive Samuel Goldwyn said one word to him, the contract would be void and he would be paid in full. Goldwyn became impatient when Hecht did not submit any material for two weeks, and, when he called to find out what was the problem, Hecht demanded $10,000 and quit work on the film.

10. **GEORGE RAFT**

George Raft wanted to get out of his contract with Warner Brothers, but he was still owed $100,000 by the studio. Jack Warner offered him a $10,000 buyout. The studio head was stunned when Raft misunderstood his offer and wrote Warner a check for $10,000.

It's Only Money

Not every movie star is paid millions of dollars per picture. Montgomery Clift waived his salary for co-starring in *Judgment at Nuremburg* as a tribute to the victims of the Holocaust. Clift sent his agent an empty paper bag as his commission on Clift's salary for the picture.

1. WILLIAM HURT

When the production of the 1985 film *Kiss of the Spider Woman* ran short of money, actor William Hurt agreed to appear in the film for no salary. Hurt was rewarded when he won the Best Actor Oscar for that year.

2. EDGAR ULMER

Director Edgar Ulmer was known for making low-budget films such as *Detour*. In 1939, Ulmer directed a film, called *Moon Over Harlem*. Fifty chorus girls were paid a dollar a week, from which they had to pay for their transportation. They all ended up losing money on the deal.

3. **FATTY ARBUCKLE**

Comedian Fatty Arbuckle was paid $3 a day as a Keystone Cop in 1913. Within a few years, he was one of the movies' most popular comedians and earned as much as $7,000 a week. Arbuckle remained one of Hollywood's highest paid stars until a 1921 scandal involving the death of actress Virginia Rappe destroyed his career.

4. **RUDOLPH VALENTINO**

Rudolph Valentino was paid only $5 a day for his first film, *Alimony* (1918). Three years later, Valentino became a star with the release of *The Four Horsemen of the Apocalypse.* The Great Lover remained one of Hollywood's most popular leading men until his untimely death in 1926.

5. **JOAN CHEN**

Joan Chen was the most popular actress in China. In 1980, Chen earned $8 a month. Since that time, the movie industry in China has prospered, and salaries have risen.

6. **PRESTON STURGES**

Preston Sturges was a successful screenwriter during the 1930s. He wanted to direct films as well and made a deal with the studio. He agreed to accept only $10 for the script for his film, *The Great McGinty* (1940), on the condition that he be allowed to direct. Sturges won the Academy Award for best screenplay, and *The Great McGinty* was the first of Sturges's comic masterpieces, which include *Sullivan's Travels* and *The Palm Beach Story.*

7. TERESA IZEWSKA

Teresa Izewska, star of the film classic *Kanal* (1957), was paid $12 a month by the Polish government. Izewska also received a dress and a pair of shoes so she could attend a film festival where the movie was being shown.

8. ROBERT DE NIRO

Robert De Niro, a two-time Academy Award winner and one of Hollywood's most acclaimed actors, was paid $50 for his first role, in *The Wedding Party*. The film was shot in 1963 but wasn't released until six years later, and De Niro's name was misspelled "De Nero" in the credits.

9. MARILYN MONROE

In 1949, Marilyn Monroe was paid $50 for posing nude for a calendar. Four years later, one of the photos was used for the centerfold in the first issue of *Playboy* magazine; publisher Hugh Hefner paid $500 for the rights to use it. The photo helped launch *Playboy*, one of magazine publishing's greatest success stories. The calendar company earned more than $750,000 from the Monroe photos.

10. ELI WALLACH

Eli Wallach was paid $350 to play Mr. Freeze in the 1960s cult television series, *Batman.* By contrast, Arnold Schwarzenegger was paid $25 million for his screen portrayal of Mr. Freeze in the 1997 film *Batman and Robin.*

Memorable Memorabilia

The demand for star memorabilia has increased dramatically over the last 30 years. Almost anything seen in a film or owned by a star is considered collectible and valuable. At a 1978 auction, a pair of loaded dice given to Judy Garland by Frank Sinatra sold for $1,200. The loincloth worn by Charlton Heston in *Ben Hur* sold for $10,000. Two-time Academy Award–winning actor Kevin Spacey paid $156,875 at a September 2001 auction for an Oscar won by composer George Stoll for his score for the 1945 film *Anchors Aweigh*. Spacey presented the award to the Motion Picture Academy.

1. MARILYN MONROE

Marilyn Monroe memorabilia is highly collectible. In 1999, collectors paid more than $13 million for 1,000 items owned by Monroe. One collector paid $1.26 million for the form-fitting rhinestone dress Monroe wore when she sang "Happy Birthday" to President John Kennedy in 1962. The eternity band Joe DiMaggio gave Marilyn brought $772,500. Designer Tommy

Hilfiger paid $42,550 for three pairs of blue jeans she wore in *The Misfits*.

2. ELVIS PRESLEY

In 1995, at an auction of Elvis Presley memorabilia at the Las Vegas Hilton, collectors paid $2,365,837 for 617 items. A faux turquoise jumpsuit sold for $101,500; Presley's birth certificate brought a bid of $68,500; his American Express credit card was purchased for $41,400; and his plastic comb went for $1,092.

3. MICHAEL JACKSON

On June 12, 1999, Michael Jackson paid $1.5 million for the Best Picture Oscar given to producer David O. Selznick for *Gone With the Wind*. The Oscar was 1 of 10 the film received in 1940.

4. JUDY GARLAND

In 1970, MGM auctioned off a pair of the ruby slippers worn by Judy Garland in *The Wizard of Oz* for $15,000. Eighteen years later, the ruby slippers sold for $165,000 at a Christie's auction. By 2000, the price of the ruby slippers had escalated to $666,000.

5. STEVEN SPIELBERG

In 1982, Steven Spielberg paid $60,500 for the Rosebud sled from *Citizen Kane*. In 1996, Spielberg paid $607,500 for the Best Actor Oscar Clark Gable won for his performance in the 1934 film *It Happened One Night*. Spielberg returned the Oscar to the Academy of Motion Picture Arts and Sciences.

Five years later, Spielberg paid $570,000 for Bette Davis's Best Actress Oscar won in 1938 for her performance in *Jezebel.* Once again, Spielberg presented the Oscar to AMPAS.

6. VIVIEN LEIGH

The Oscar won by Vivien Leigh for her portrayal of Scarlett O'Hara in *Gone With the Wind* was auctioned for $560,000 at a Sotheby auction in 1993. Leigh, who died in 1967, won a second Oscar for her performance as Blanche du Bois in the 1952 film *A Streetcar Named Desire.*

7. CHARLIE CHAPLIN

At a 1987 Christie's auction in London, the bowler and cane used by Charlie Chaplin in his comedies sold for $150,000. The items were part of the outfit worn by Chaplin's "Little Tramp," a character Chaplin portrayed in films for more than 20 years.

8. URSULA ANDRESS

The white bikini worn by Ursula Andress in the James Bond film *Dr. No* sold for $59,782 at a Christie's auction. The revealing outfit had helped launch Andress's career as an international sex symbol.

9. DOROTHY LAMOUR

In a 1970s auction of celebrity memorabilia, a sarong worn by Dorothy Lamour in one of the Bob Hope–Bing Crosby *Road* pictures sold for $50,000. Lamour appeared in *Road to Singapore, Road to Zanzibar, Road to Morocco, Road to Utopia, Road to Rio, Road to Bali,* and *Road to Hong Kong.*

10. **BERT LAHR**

At the end of the 1939 film *The Wizard of Oz,* the Cowardly Lion, portrayed by Bert Lahr, was presented with a medal of courage. In 1999, the medal sold for $33,350 at a Sotheby's auction.

Sign In Please

F ans covet the autographs of their favorite stars. Before he became a star, Tony Curtis sold forged autographs of actress Deanna Durbin. Robert Mitchum sometimes signed Kirk Douglas's name when asked for his autograph.

1. SHIRLEY TEMPLE

Shirley Temple was the most popular child star of all time. When she was six years old, she said she stopped believing in Santa Claus when a department store Santa asked for her autograph.

2. ERROL FLYNN

At the height of his popularity as a movie star, Errol Flynn was pulled over by a New York policeman. Flynn said the police officer demanded an autograph. When the actor refused, according to Flynn, he was beaten and spent a night in jail.

3. DREW BARRYMORE

Drew Barrymore was arrested for cocaine possession when she was 14 years old. She was surprised when one of the arresting officers removed her handcuffs and asked for an autograph.

4. **PAUL NEWMAN**

Paul Newman said he stopped signing autographs after someone asked him to sign while he was standing at a urinal in a restaurant bathroom. Joan Collins had a similar experience; she was seated in a toilet stall when someone shoved a piece of paper and a pen for her autograph under the stall door.

5. **RICKY NELSON**

At his peak, in the early 1960s, Ricky Nelson was second only to Elvis Presley as a teen idol. Like many rock and roll stars, Nelson went into films. His most notable role was as a young gunslinger in the 1959 western *Rio Bravo.* Nelson recalled an odd autograph request from a fan: the man asked Nelson to sign his penis. Nelson initialed it because his signature wouldn't fit.

6. **KATHARINE HEPBURN**

When Katharine Hepburn refused to sign an autograph for a fan in Central Park, the perturbed fan said, "Thanks anyway, Audrey," referring to another actress, Audrey Hepburn.

7. **GIULIETTA MASINA**

Giulietta Masina, wife of famed director Federico Fellini, starred in many of her husband's greatest films, including *La Strada* and *Nights of Cabiria.* She admitted the main reason she appeared in the 1969 film *The Madwoman of Chaillot,* was to get costar Katharine Hepburn's autograph.

8. **SPENCER TRACY**

Clark Gable and Spencer Tracy co-starred in the 1938 film *Test Pilot*. Outside the MGM studio gate, fans mobbed Clark Gable for his autograph while they completely ignored the three-time Oscar winner, Tracy. Tracy saluted Gable, saying, "Long live the King!"

9. **ZSA ZSA GABOR**

One evening Zsa Zsa and her husband, George Sanders, were walking down a street in Hollywood when a pair of teenagers recognized Zsa Zsa. They asked Gabor for her autograph. One of the girls asked Sanders, an Oscar-winning actor, his name. Gabor recalled that when she saw Sanders's expression, she knew the days of her marriage were numbered.

10. **NORMA TALMADGE**

Norma Talmadge was a major silent film star who did not make the transition to sound films. After she had retired from acting, a fan asked her for an autograph as she was leaving a restaurant. "Go away, I don't need you anymore," Talmadge said in response.

Film Fanatics

Fans often behave strangely when they meet their favorite stars. An admirer of Woody Allen stopped the actor on the street and kept saying, "You're a star! You're a star!" Allen replied, "But what will I be next year, a black hole?"

1. CARROLL BAKER

Actress Carroll Baker created a sensation with her role as a nymphet in *Baby Doll* (1957). A Masai chieftain was so smitten by the blonde sex symbol that he offered 150 cows, 200 goats, and $750 in cash for her hand in marriage. It was an impressive gesture, considering that a Masai warrior rarely offered more than a dozen cows and $200 for a wife. Despite the generous offer, Baker turned down the proposal.

2. MILTON BERLE

Comedian Milton Berle was rumored to have the largest penis in Hollywood. Once, at the Luxor Baths in New York, a stranger bet Berle $100 that he had a larger sexual organ. One of Berle's friends prodded him, "Just take out enough to win."

3. **NORMA SHEARER**

With fans like Norma Shearer's, who needed enemies? Shearer was one of the biggest stars of the 1930s. Married to MGM executive Irving Thalberg, she had the pick of the studio's choice roles. When the search for an actress to play Scarlett O'Hara in *Gone With the Wind* began, Shearer was the leading candidate. Shearer removed herself from consideration when many of her fans wrote urging her not to play the part. Most of them said she was too ladylike to play the fiery Southern belle. Little-known Vivien Leigh got the part and won an Oscar for her performance. Shearer retired a few years later.

4. **WALLACE REID**

Wallace Reid, Paramount's most popular star of the early 1900s, was one of the handsomest actors in silent films. His female admirers would do almost anything to get near him. A New York debutante once traded an emerald necklace for a peek into the handsome actor's dressing room.

5. **JAYNE MANSFIELD**

In 1959, Jayne Mansfield was in Rio de Janeiro, Brazil, for Carnaval when her fans got a little carried away. While Mansfield was performing a provocative dance, men began picking red roses from the bosom of her dress. When all the roses were plucked, the men began tearing off her clothes. By the time Mansfield escaped the mob, she was topless.

6. **ADAM SANDLER**

According to Adam Sandler, he had an encounter with a not-too-bright fan at a New Hampshire pizza parlor. The teenager told the comedian he looked just like Adam Sandler. "Yeah I know," Sandler replied. "What's your name?" the fan asked. "Adam Sandler." The amazed fan exclaimed, "Whoa, what a coincidence!"

7. ROSIE O'DONNELL

A fan met Rosie O'Donnell, the talk show host and star of the movie version of *The Flintstones,* in a store. The female customer said, "I hope you're not insulted, but you look just like Rosie O'Donnell." The comedienne replied, "I am now."

8. SHIRLEY TEMPLE

Seventeen-year-old Shirley Temple married actor John Agar on September 19, 1945, at the Wilshire Methodist Church in Los Angeles. The former child star had hoped for a quiet, old-fashioned wedding. Her plans went awry when 12,000 fans crashed the wedding, mobbing bridesmaids and tearing their blue organza dresses to pieces for souvenirs. The bride and groom escaped out a side door of the church.

9. JOAN COLLINS

Some people will do anything to dig up dirt on a star. In 1987, Joan Collins began having her garbage shredded after a trash collector began selling Collins's trash to her fans.

10. THEDA BARA

Silent film star Theda Bara was the movies' first femme fatale. It was believed that Bara had a mysterious power over men. One day, a group of women saw Bara pick up and try on a hat in a department store. Windows were broken and merchandise strewn across the floor as a mob of women tried to get the hat Bara had touched.

Hollywood
Name Game

M ost actors are not born with a name befitting a movie star. One of the first steps a studio took when transforming someone into a star was to change the person's name. Some actresses were born with names that did not enhance their marketability: Sandra Zuck became Sandra Dee. Other actors had foreign names that were difficult to remember. Ted Knight's real name was Tadewurz Wladziv Konopka, Danny Thomas was born Muzyad Yakhoob, and Dirk Bogarde's full name was Derek Julius Gaspard Ulrich Niven van den Bogaerde.

1. ALBERT BROOKS

Albert Brooks is an Oscar-nominated actor and the director of films such as *Real Life* and *Lost in America.* His real name was Albert Einstein, the same as the discoverer of the theory of relativity. Brooks changed his name in honor of another comic genius, Mel Brooks.

2. CYD CHARISSE

Cyd Charisse displayed her dancing skills in *Singin' in the Rain, The Band Wagon,* and many other Hollywood musicals.

Her lovely legs were insured for $5 million. Her real name, Tula Elice Finklea, was hardly suitable for a screen siren.

3. JOAN CRAWFORD

Joan Crawford's real name was Lucille Le Sueur. She changed her name because MGM studio boss Louis B. Mayer thought it sounded too much like "sewer." Crawford went on to become one of Hollywood's most enduring stars.

4. JACK LEMMON

Jack Lemmon's real name was Jack Lemmon. Columbia's Harry Cohn urged him to change his name: "They'll kill you," Cohn said to Lemmon. "They'll say Lemmon is a lemon." Lemmon insisted on keeping his name, went on to win two Academy Awards, and became one of the most respected actors in Hollywood.

5. CARY GRANT

Suave Cary Grant was one of Hollywood's most popular leading men. The debonair actor starred in such film classics as *Holiday, The Philadelphia Story,* and *North by Northwest.* It's hard to imagine his career being as successful if he had kept his real name, Archibald Alexander Leach.

6. WALTER MATTHAU

Walter Matthau is best remembered for his roles in *The Odd Couple* and *The Fortune Cookie.* Matthau's real name, Walter Matuschanskayasky, would not have fit on the movie marquee.

7. KIRK DOUGLAS

Another actor with a name that was a mouthful was Kirk Douglas. The star of *Lust for Life, Paths of Glory,* and *Spartacus* was born Issur Danielovitch, later changed to Isidore Demsky.

8. RUDOLPH VALENTINO

The actor with the longest name was silent film star Rudolph Valentino. Valentino's full name was Rodolfo Alfonzo Raffaele Pierre Philibert Guglielmi di Valentine Antonguolla.

9. GRETA GARBO

Studio executives at MGM did not like the sound of Greta Garbo's name. Her real name was Greta Gustafsson, but she had taken the name Garbo as an actress in Europe. Louis B. Mayer thought the name sounded too much like "garbage." It was suggested that she change her name to Mona Gabor. Years later, the Gabor sisters, Zsa Zsa and Eva, made the name famous.

10. JUDY GARLAND

Frances Gumm performed as a child with her two sisters in a singing act known as the Gumm Sisters. Entertainer George Jessel suggested they change their name—or be referred to as the Glum Sisters or the Dumb Sisters. Frances eventually changed her name to Judy Garland. "Judy" was in honor of a Hoagy Carmichael song, and "Garland" was inspired by a critic named Robert Garland.

Rip, Chill, and Twinkle

Sometimes actors' names are changed to make them more memorable. Here are 10 of Hollywood's strangest names.

1. MINK STOLE

Mink Stole appeared in several John Waters movies. She portrayed a mental patient in *Mondo Trasho* and *Desperate Living* and competed with Divine for the title of the "filthiest human being on the face of the earth" in *Pink Flamingos.*

2. RIP TORN

Veteran character actor Rip Torn has one of Hollywood's most original names. Some of Torn's best-known movies are *Cross Creek, The Cincinnati Kid,* and *Tropic of Cancer.* His real name was Elmore Torn.

3. SLIM PICKENS

Character actor Slim Pickens spoofed his image as a star of westerns in the Mel Brooks comedy *Blazing Saddles.* He is best remembered for his role of Major Kong, who rides a nuclear bomb like a bucking bronco, in *Dr. Strangelove.* Pickens's real name was Louis Bert Lindley, Jr.

4. STEPIN FETCHIT

Stepin Fetchit was a black supporting actor in the 1930s who appeared in four films with humorist Will Rogers. He got his unusual name from a vaudeville act in which he performed a number, called "Step and Fetch It." His real name was Lincoln Theodore Monroe Andrew Perry. He had been named for four American presidents: Abraham Lincoln, Theodore Roosevelt, James Monroe, and Andrew Jackson.

5. SLEEP 'N EAT

Another African-American comedian of the 1930s was Sleep 'n Eat. He felt that the name was demeaning, and, in 1936, he convinced the studio to permit him to appear in films under his real name, Willie Best.

6. TWINKLE WATTS

Twinkle Watts was Republic Pictures' answer to Shirley Temple. The child actress never caught on, and she retired from motion pictures at age eight.

7. CASH FLAGG

Ray Dennis Steckler directed some of the worst films ever made, including *Rat Pfink a Boo Boo* and *The Incredibly Strange Creatures Who Stopped Living and Became Mixed-Up Zombies.* Steckler starred in several of his films under the name Cash Flagg.

8. SIMONE SIMON

French actress Simone Simon is best remembered today for her distinctive name. Her best-known film, *Cat People,* was released in 1942. In it she played a character who turned into a panther. One of her contract demands at Fox was that she be given her own panther. She said, "I like to have wild things around me, and he'll look beautiful when I take him shopping with me."

9. HELEN TWELVETREES

Another actress with an unforgettable name was Helen Twelvetrees. Born Helen Jurgens, she married artist Clark Twelvetrees in 1927. During the 1930s, she starred in a number of tearjerkers.

10. CHILL WILLS

Chill Wills had a long career as a character actor. He was the original voice of Francis the Talking Mule, and, in 1960, he was nominated for a Best Supporting Actor Oscar for his performance in *The Alamo*.

No Publicity Is Bad Publicity

It has been said that even bad publicity is better than no publicity at all. For more than 30 years, publisher William Randolph Hearst insisted that in his newspapers there be at least one mention every day of his mistress, Marion Davies. From 1922 to 1934, the Western Association of Motion Picture Advertisers (WAMPAS) sponsored a bizarre annual promotion in which the most promising new female stars were dressed as babies and posed for publicity shots. Ads for the 1945 film *Mildred Pierce* read, "Don't tell what Mildred Pierce did." An enterprising owner of a Los Angeles diner ran an ad that said, "For 65 cents we'll not only serve you a swell blue plate special, we'll tell you what Mildred Pierce did."

1. JAYNE MANSFIELD

No one sought publicity more than Jayne Mansfield; Bob Hope said she absorbed publicity like a sponge. Mansfield said that one of her goals was to have her own billboard.

She said, "Publicity can be terrible, but only if you don't have any." She opened supermarkets and once made an appearance at a butcher shop in exchange for 250 pounds of meat.

Mansfield loved to upstage other sex symbols. One of her most famous stunts occurred at a party at Romanoff's, given in honor of Sophia Loren. Mansfield, who sat next to Loren, was wearing a dress cut so low that her nipples were visible. A famous photo shows Loren staring at Mansfield's cleavage. Jayne told the press it was the only dress that she had that wasn't at the cleaners. Another time, producer Howard Hughes arranged for a photo shoot with star Jane Russell for his film, *Underwater.* Hughes arranged for the voluptuous Russell to be photographed underwater. Mansfield stole the spotlight by diving into the pool and conveniently losing her bikini top.

2. **JANE RUSSELL**

Jane Russell became famous because of the publicity campaign for her film, *The Outlaw.* Producer Howard Hughes hired publicist Russell Birdwell to create interest in the western. For two years, Hughes withheld release of the film so he could carry out an unprecedented publicity campaign. When the film was released in 1943, Birdwell advertised it with a billboard depicting a scantily clad Russell, with the slogan, "How would you like to tussle with Russell?" At the Hollywood premiere, Birdwell hired skywriters to write two large circles with dots in the center as a not-too-subtle reminder of the star's greatest physical attributes. According to Hughes, there were "two good reasons why men will go see her."

3. DOUGLAS FAIRBANKS

Douglas Fairbanks shot an arrow into the air, and it landed in someone's derriere. As a publicity stunt for his 1921 film, *Robin Hood,* Fairbanks shot an arrow from a New York City rooftop. A tailor across the street, struck in the rear by the errant arrow, received a $5,000 settlement.

4. TOM MIX

Cowboy star Tom Mix fabricated his past to coincide with his heroic film persona. Mix claimed to have been one of Teddy Roosevelt's Rough Riders, fought on both sides of the Boer War, and participated in the Boxer Rebellion. He marketed a foldout chart to his young fans that showed the location of 21 bullet and knife wounds Mix incurred during his adventures.

5. RUDOLPH VALENTINO

In 1926, Rudolph Valentino died suddenly at the age of 31. Female fans around the world mourned his passing. Publicist Russell Birdwell concocted a stunt that would add to Valentino's aura after his death. On the first anniversary of Valentino's death, Birdwell hired an actress to dress in black and lay flowers at the actor's tomb. The following year, Birdwell was astonished when a mysterious veiled lady in black visited the tomb. The woman, Ditra Flame, laid a dozen red roses and a single white rose at Valentino's tomb for many years on the anniversary of his death.

6. FRANCIS X. BUSHMAN

Francis X. Bushman, the star of the silent epic *Ben Hur,* was involved in one of the strangest publicity stunts of all time. During the Depression, his press agent, Harry Reichenbach, instructed him to fill his pockets with nickels. Bushman walked through the city, dropping the coins from holes in his pockets. As planned, a crowd began following the star around town.

7. GERTA ROZEN

Russell Birdwell would do anything to create interest in a film. To promote *So Ends the Night,* he instructed Gerta Rozen, an actress with a small part in the film, to call a press conference during which she would take off a different item of clothing every day until she was given a bigger part in the film. To the reporters' disappointment, Rozen never did take it all off.

8. PINOCCHIO

At the New York premiere of the 1940 Disney animated classic, *Pinocchio,* a publicity stunt went terribly awry. Eleven midgets sang and danced atop the theater marquee. The idea was to entertain the children waiting in line to see the film. Unfortunately, some of the midgets amused themselves by drinking gin and whiskey. Soon the tipsy midgets began making wisecracks at the children and performing a strip show. Other midgets passed the time by playing craps. The drunken display ended when the police carted off the midgets.

9. *THE MAN I KILLED*

A publicity stunt for the 1932 film *The Man I Killed* almost proved deadly. The stunt, burying a man alive, was supposed to last 24 hours. Unfortunately, a storm washed away the grave marker. Thirty men desperately dug to locate the man before his oxygen ran out. He was rescued just in time, and, as soon as the man caught his breath, he demanded overtime.

10. **FROZEN ASSETS**

In the 1992 film *Frozen Assets,* Corbin Bernsen played the president of a sperm bank. The producers the film announced a Stud of the Year contest that offered a Caribbean cruise to the man with the highest sperm count.

Smarter than the Average Bara

D irector George Cukor once said, "Never underestimate the stupidity of actors." Actually, many actors are highly intelligent. James Stewart graduated from Princeton with a degree in architecture. Elizabeth Shue studied English and political science at Wellesley. Tommy Lee Jones was former Vice President Al Gore's roommate at Harvard. Kris Kristofferson was a Rhodes Scholar at Oxford and taught English at West Point. The grandfather of Jordana Brewster was president of Yale, the university she attends. Sigourney Weaver attended Yale and Stanford and earned a master's degree in fine arts. Other actors with an Ivy League education include Jennifer Connelly, Lisa Kudrow, Dean Cain, Jack Lemmon, Meryl Streep, James Whitmore, Sam Waterston, Christopher Reeve, Brooke Shields, and Stacy Keach.

1. JAMES WOODS

Possibly Hollywood's most cerebral actor, James Woods was a straight-A student in high school. He scored a genius-level 180 on an IQ test. Woods attended the Massachusetts Institute of Technology as a political science major, specializing in national defense analysis.

2. **DAVID DUCHOVNY**

The star of *The X-Files,* David Duchovny attended Princeton University and received a master's degree from Yale. While Duchovny was working on his doctorate (his Ph.D. thesis was titled "Magic and Technology in Contemporary Fiction"), he landed his first acting job, a Lowenbrau beer commercial.

3. **HEDY LAMARR**

Hedy Lamarr was considered one of the most beautiful actresses in film history, and she was also one of the brainiest. During World War II, she patented the process of frequency hopping. Lamarr believed the new technology could be used in launching torpedoes from submarines. Years later, her discovery became widely used in cell phone technology. Lamarr always downplayed her intellect, saying, "Anyone can look glamorous. All you have to do is stand still and look stupid."

4. **JODIE FOSTER**

Two-time Oscar winner Jodie Foster attended the Los Angeles Lycée Français, where only French was spoken. Foster gave her valedictory speech in French and English, and she graduated magna cum laude from Yale.

5. **JOHN LITHGOW**

Emmy winner John Lithgow graduated magna cum laude from Harvard. The star of *The World According to Garp* and *Terms of Endearment* studied under a Fulbright fellowship at The London Academy of Music and Dramatic Art.

6. **VINCENT PRICE**

Vincent Price starred in a number of acclaimed dramas, including *Laura* and *The Song of Bernadette,* but he became more famous for his horror films *(The House on Haunted Hill* and *The Masque of the Red Death).* Educated at Yale and the University of London, Price was an art expert and collector. He bought his first Rembrandt etching at age 13.

7. **ROBERT SHAW**

Robert Shaw is best known for his role as the sea captain obsessed with the great white shark in *Jaws.* Shaw was also an acclaimed novelist who was awarded the prestigious Hawthornden Prize in 1962. His novels include *The Hiding Place, The Man in the Glass Booth,* and *The Sun Doctor.*

8. **MIRA SORVINO**

Mira Sorvino won an Academy Award for her supporting actress performance as a dim-witted prostitute in *Mighty Aphrodite.* Unlike her most famous role, Sorvino is very intelligent; she graduated magna cum laude from Harvard with a degree in East Asian studies.

9. **ALLY SHEEDY**

Ally Sheedy was a member of the Brat Pack, a young group of actors in the 1980s that included Demi Moore, Rob Lowe, and Molly Ringwald, among others. Sheedy's mother is well-known literary agent Charlotte Sheedy. At age 12, Ally was a literary prodigy and published her first book, a best-selling children's work, entitled *She Looks Nice to Mice.* As a teenager she published short stories and wrote film reviews for *The Village Voice.*

10. **BUDDY EBSEN**

Buddy Ebsen had a long career in films before gaining greater fame on television. Ebsen was the original choice to play the Tin Man in *The Wizard of Oz,* but he was replaced by Jack Haley when he suffered a serious allergic reaction to the silver makeup. His most famous role was as Jed Clampett on the long-running sitcom, *The Beverly Hillbillies.* Unlike the simple backwoodsman he played on television, Ebsen is very intelligent. In 1994, at age 86, he published his autobiography, *The Other Side of Oz,* and he was 93 when he published his novel, *Kelly's Quest.*

The Write Stuff

O ver the years, many major authors have written
screenplays for movies. The great playwright George
Bernard Shaw won an Academy Award in 1938 for the
screen adaptation of *Pygmalion*. Other notable authors who
worked in Hollywood include Aldous Huxley, Raymond
Chandler, Arthur Miller, and Dorothy Parker.

1. SAM SHEPARD

Sam Shepard, whose best-known play is *True West*, is one of
America's premier playwrights. Shepard has acted, written
screenplays, and directed films; he starred in the critically
acclaimed *Days of Heaven* and received an Oscar nomination
for his portrayal of test pilot Chuck Yeager in *The Right Stuff*.
Shepard also has had a long romantic relationship with
Oscar-winning actress Jessica Lange.

2. MICHAEL CRICHTON

Michael Crichton is the author of many best sellers that have
been turned into successful movies, including *Jurassic Park*
and *Congo*. Also a successful director, Crichton's film credits
include *Westworld* and *Looker*.

3. **NORMAN MAILER**

Major literary figure Norman Mailer's celebrated works include *The Naked and the Dead, The Deer Park,* and *The Executioner's Song.* In addition to his literary achievements, Mailer directed four films: *Wild 90, Beyond the Law, Maidstone,* and *Tough Guys Don't Dance.*

4. **TRUMAN CAPOTE**

Acclaimed novelist Truman Capote's best seller, *In Cold Blood,* was made into a movie starring Robert Blake. Capote's attitude toward Hollywood was part fascination, part contempt. He said that a person lost one IQ point every year he spent in California. Although Capote was quoted as saying that actors were stupid, he did try his hand at acting: in 1976, he portrayed an eccentric millionaire in the film, *Murder by Death.*

5. **F. SCOTT FITZGERALD**

One of America's greatest novelists, F. Scott Fitzgerald wrote *The Great Gatsby* and *Tender Is the Night.* When his popularity as a novelist began to wane in the 1930s, he went to Hollywood to earn a living as a screenwriter. Although Fitzgerald had three stints in Hollywood, he was only given screen credit for one film, the 1938 drama *Three Comrades.* Fitzgerald's Hollywood career was hindered by his excessive drinking; at a party hosted by actress Norma Shearer, a drunken Fitzgerald sang incessantly to a dog. Fitzgerald died of heart attack on December 21, 1940, at the age of 44. At the time of his death, he was working on a novel about Hollywood, titled *The Last Tycoon.* Fitzgerald's book royalties during the last year of his life were only $13.

6. **WILLIAM FAULKNER**

Another brilliant novelist who worked as a screenwriter was William Faulkner. The Nobel Prize–winning author penned such classics as *The Sound and the Fury* and *Absalom, Absalom.* Faulkner's off-and-on career as a screenwriter lasted from the early 1930s to the mid-1950s. His screen credits included the Humphrey Bogart films *To Have and Have Not* and *The Big Sleep.* In 1932, Faulkner went on a hunting trip with director Howard Hawks and actor Clark Gable. Gable, who had never heard of Faulkner, asked him, "Do you write?" The author replied, "Yes, Mr. Gable. What do you do?" Years later Faulkner was given a huge office by studio head Jack Warner. However, when Faulkner asked if he could write at home, Warner agreed, only to discover later that Faulkner had returned home to Oxford, Mississippi.

7. **GORE VIDAL**

Gore Vidal is best known for his series of historical novels about America. One of the most successful of Vidal's screen adaptations was the 1960 political drama, *The Best Man.* Vidal was known to disown films he worked on when the final product was not up to his standards. Two of the films Vidal disowned were *Myra Breckenridge* and *Billy the Kid.*

8. **JOHN STEINBECK**

Several of John Steinbeck's novels were made into well-received movies. Two of the best films adapted from his novels were *The Grapes of Wrath* and *East of Eden.* Steinbeck also wrote several screenplays, most notably, *The Red Pony* and *Viva Zapata.* One afternoon Steinbeck was in the office of Darryl F. Zanuck discussing the possibility of making a film of Steinbeck's novel, *The Grapes of Wrath*. Suddenly, a secretary rushed into the office and informed Zanuck that Shirley Temple had lost a front tooth. Frantically, Zanuck tried to figure out what to do about his child star. Steinbeck excused himself, realizing *The Grapes of Wrath* was insignificant compared to Shirley Temple's tooth.

9. STEPHEN KING

Stephen King has become a virtual film industry; many of his novels and short stories have been adapted for the screen. These include the horror classics *Carrie* and *The Shining,* as well as critically acclaimed dramas such as *The Shawshank Redemption* and *The Green Mile*. King also appeared as an actor in *Creepshow* and *Pet Semetary* and has had cameos in other films adapted from his books.

10. NATHANIEL WEST

Nathaniel West, who wrote the novel *Miss Lonelyhearts,* worked on the screenplays of *It Could Happen to You, Five Came Back,* and other films in the 1930s. His novel *The Day of the Locust* is one of the best written about Hollywood. On December 13, 1940, he and his friend, F. Scott Fitzgerald, had dinner at West's home. A week later, Fitzgerald died of a heart attack. On the day after Fitzgerald's death, the 37-year-old West was killed in an automobile accident.

Music to Their Ears

Over the years many music stars have become actors. Bing Crosby, Frank Sinatra, Barbra Streisand, and Cher were singers who became Oscar winners. Occasionally actors have tried to duplicate their success in the music industry. Here are 10 of the most unlikely stars to become top 40 hit-makers.

1. WALTER BRENNAN

Three-time Oscar winner Walter Brennan was 65 years old when he recorded the first of his three top 40 hits, "Dutchman's Gold," in 1959. A year later, Brennan's "Old Rivers," about a farmer and his mule, reached number five in the hit parade.

2. LORNE GREENE

Lorne Greene appeared in many films, but is best remembered for his role as Ben Cartwright on the top-rated television show, *Bonanza*. In 1964, Greene recorded a number one hit song, "Ringo." The song was not about the Beatles' drummer; it was the story of a gunfighter named Johnny Ringo.

Some of the rock classics that ranked below "Ringo" on the charts the week it reached number one were The Zombies' "She's Not There," The Supremes' "Baby Love," The Rolling Stones' "Time Is on My Side," The Kinks' "You Really Got Me," and The Beatles' "I Feel Fine."

3. JIM BACKUS

Jim Backus starred in the James Dean film *Rebel Without a Cause,* and the television sitcoms *I Married Joan* and *Gilligan's Island.* He was best known as the voice of the near-sighted cartoon character, Mister Magoo. In 1958, Backus had a top 40 hit with the song, "Delicious!" The record label, Jubilee, spelled his name "Bakus."

4. ANTHONY PERKINS

Anthony Perkins played the deranged Norman Bates in the Alfred Hitchcock masterpiece *Psycho.* In 1957, Perkins recorded a song, "Moon-Light Swim," that reached number 24 on the charts.

5. ANDY GRIFFITH

Andy Griffith starred in the films *A Face in the Crowd* and *No Time for Sergeants,* and in the long-running series *Andy Griffith Show* and *Matlock.* In 1955, Griffith's song "Make Yourself Comfortable" was a top 40 hit.

6. BRUCE WILLIS

One of the biggest box office attractions of the 1990s, Bruce Willis has starred in action films such as *Pulp Fiction* and *Die Hard.* His 1987 recording "Respect Yourself" reached number five. Willis still performs with his band occasionally.

7. EDDIE MURPHY

Eddie Murphy has starred in a number of comic film hits, such as *Trading Places, Beverly Hills Cop,* and *The Nutty Professor.* Murphy's 1985 recording of "Party All the Time" reached number two on the Billboard charts.

8. JOHN TRAVOLTA

John Travolta, the star of *Saturday Night Fever, Look Who's Talking,* and *Pulp Fiction,* had five top 40 hits between 1976 and 1978. His duet with Olivia Newton-John, "You're the One That I Want," reached number one. The song came from *Grease,* the musical movie in which they co-starred.

9. SAL MINEO

Sal Mineo was nominated for Best Supporting Actor for his performances in *Rebel Without a Cause* (1955) and *Exodus* (1960). Mineo had a top 10 hit in 1957 with his song, "Start Movin'."

10. GEORGE MAHARIS

George Maharis played Buz Murdoch on the television series *Route 66.* He left the show after three seasons to pursue a film career. Maharis had a top 40 hit in 1962 with his version of "Teach Me Tonight."

The Candidates

Ronald Reagan was not the only actor to become a politician. Many movie stars have served as mayors: Will Rogers (Beverly Hills), Charles Farrell (Palm Springs), Al Jolson (Encino), Martin Sheen (Malibu), Jack Kelly (Huntington Beach), and Clint Eastwood (Carmel). In 1938, director Cecil B. De Mille was offered the Republican nomination for the U.S. Senate from California, but he declined to run. Edward Arnold, a character actor who appeared in such films as *Easy Living, Mr. Smith Goes to Washington,* and *Meet John Doe,* ran for the Senate in California, only to lose to future President Richard Nixon.

1. RONALD REAGAN

Between 1937 and 1964, Ronald Reagan starred in dozens of films, ranging from the exceptional *(Kings Row)* to the forgettable *(Bedtime for Bonzo).* In 1942, *Kings Row* costar Robert Cummings told the young Reagan, "You ought to run for president." Reagan replied, "Don't you like my acting either?" Reagan was elected governor of California in 1966 and served as president of the United States from 1981 to 1989.

2. JESSE VENTURA

Jesse "The Body" Ventura gained fame as a professional wrestler before turning to acting. He appeared in a number of films, most notably, *Predator* and *The Running Man.* In 1998, Ventura stunned the political world by winning the governorship of Minnesota on the Reform Party ticket.

3. GEORGE MURPHY

George Murphy played Ronald Reagan's father in the 1942 film, *This Is the Army,* and he appeared in nearly 40 films before becoming a politician. Murphy was elected to the U.S. Senate from California in 1964 and served one term.

4. JOHN LODGE

A leading man in the 1930s, John Lodge starred in such films as *Little Women* and *The Scarlet Empress.* Lodge also had a long and distinguished career in politics. He was elected to the U.S. House of Representatives (1946) and as governor of Connecticut (1950) and later served as U.S. ambassador to Spain, Argentina, and Switzerland.

5. HELEN GAHAGAN DOUGLAS

Helen Gahagan starred in just one film, *She,* in 1935. Married to actor Melvyn Douglas, she retired from acting and went into politics. During the 1940s, she was elected as a congresswoman in California's 14th district. Her greatest notoriety came in the hotly contested 1950 U.S. Senate race. Her opponent, Richard Nixon, depicted Douglas as being soft on communism. Nixon won the election and, two years later, became the vice president of the United States.

6. FRED GRANDY

Fred Grandy was a film and television actor best known for his role as "Gopher" on the television series *The Love Boat.* From 1986 to 1995, Grandy served as a congressman for the state of Iowa. He also made an unsuccessful bid for that state's governorship.

7. SHIRLEY TEMPLE

Shirley Temple, the most popular child star of the 1930s, retired from acting at an early age and began a career in politics. In 1968, Shirley Temple Black ran for the congressional seat from California's 12th district, but lost to Paul McCloskey. One of her campaign posters had a photo of a 10-year-old Shirley Temple with the slogan, "If you don't vote for me, I'll hold my breath." Richard Nixon appointed her U.S. representative to the United Nations. Black served as an U.S. ambassador to Ghana from 1974 to 1976, when she became U.S. Chief of Protocol.

8. BEN JONES

Ben Jones, a veteran film character actor, played Cooter on the television series, *The Dukes of Hazzard.* Jones was elected to Congress representing Georgia's Fourth District in 1988.

9. SONNY BONO

Sonny Bono recorded the hit *I Got You Babe* with his then-wife, Cher. They starred in their own television series, *The Sonny and Cher Comedy Hour,* and he appeared as a mad bomber in the film comedy *Airplane II.* Bono was elected mayor of Palm Springs, California, in 1988 and later served as a congressman representing California.

10. **REX BELL**

Rex Bell, who starred in westerns during the 1930s, married silent film star Clara Bow in 1931. In 1954, he was elected lieutenant governor of Nevada; he was running for governor in 1962 when he suffered a fatal heart attack.

Party Animals

Some Hollywood parties never seemed to end. Kirk Douglas used to put on his pajamas to demonstrate to party guests that they had overstayed their welcome. Barbara Stanwyck described bad Hollywood parties as "fêtes worse than death." Groucho Marx once told a hostess, "I've had a wonderful evening, but this wasn't it."

1. MARION DAVIES

Costume parties were extremely popular during the Golden Age of Hollywood. One of the most memorable of these was thrown by Marion Davies in 1926 in the Ambassador Hotel ballroom. Mary Pickford came as fellow actress Lillian Gish, Charlie Chaplin was dressed as Napoleon, and John Gilbert masqueraded as football star Red Grange. John Barrymore's tramp costume was so convincing he had trouble getting into the party.

2. WILLIAM RANDOLPH HEARST

The parties at publisher William Randolph Hearst's palatial estate, Sam Simeon, were legendary, and were attended by

Hollywood's biggest stars. The parties usually had a theme: Hearst's 70th birthday party's was pioneers. Norma Shearer, who relished standing out from the crowd, ignored the pioneer theme and came as Marie Antoinette. At a 1937 circus costume party, Bette Davis appeared as a bearded lady.

3. **BASIL RATHBONE**

To celebrate his 11th anniversary, Basil Rathbone threw a bride and groom costume party. Two hundred fifty guests came dressed as famous couples such as Romeo and Juliet and Napoleon and Josephine. The strangest costume belonged to Loretta Young, who came alone as Mrs. Satan.

4. **BETTE DAVIS**

In the late 1930s, Bette Davis organized the Tailwagger's Ball. The purpose of the event, held at the Hollywood Hotel, was to raise money for an animal shelter and to train seeing-eye dogs for the blind. Among the stars in attendance were Jimmy Stewart, Errol Flynn, Norma Shearer, and Joel McCrea. A late-arriving guest was producer Howard Hughes, who came dressed in a rumpled tuxedo.

5. **PIMMIE NIVEN**

A 1946 party thrown by Tyrone Power turned deadly. The all-star guest list included Clark Gable, Rex Harrison, and Gene Tierney. David Niven came with his 28-year-old wife, Pimmie. After dinner, some of the guests played Sardines, a form of hide-and-seek. Pimmie Niven went off to hide, and she mistook the door to the basement steps for a closet. Niven fell down the steps and suffered a fatal skull fracture.

6. CECIL B. DE MILLE

When director Cecil B. De Mille gave lavish dinner parties at his ranch house, known as Paradise, he frequently placed gifts next to the women's place settings. Female guests often received bottles of perfume specially made from flowers grown on the ranch. After dinner, he escorted the women to his billiard room and instructed each guest to roll a ball on the table to determine the order guests would choose their party gifts. A valet brought the gifts, which could be anything from cosmetics to costume jewelry. Occasionally De Mille placed a precious gem in one of the gift boxes.

7. MIKE TODD

On October 17, 1957, producer Mike Todd threw a fabulous party at Madison Square Garden to celebrate the first anniversary of his Academy Award–winning film, *Around the World in 80 Days.* The marquee read, "CLOSED FOR A LITTLE PRIVATE PARTY." In fact, 18,000 guests jammed the arena, and more than 35 million watched the party on television.

8. MARILYN MONROE

On May 19, 1962, Madison Square Garden was the site of President John Kennedy's 45th birthday party. The highlight of the evening was an appearance by Marilyn Monroe. As usual, Monroe was late to arrive; when she did, Peter Lawford introduced her as "the late Marilyn Monroe." Wearing a skin-tight gown designed by Jean-Louis, she sang a breathless version of "Happy Birthday." Kennedy joked later, "I can now retire from politics having "Happy Birthday" sung to me in such a sweet, wholesome way." At the time few knew that Monroe and Kennedy reportedly had carried on a clandestine affair.

9. **AL CAPONE**

Scarface, the 1932 gangster classic directed by Howard Hawks, was based loosely on the life of Al Capone. Scarface Al showed there were no hard feelings by throwing a party for the cast and crew.

10. **NORMA SHEARER**

Norma Shearer had the reputation of being one of Hollywood's best hostesses. In 1939, she threw a party at which Douglas Fairbanks was supposed to be the guest of honor. When Fairbanks did not appear, guests were not told the reason. The truth was that Fairbanks had died that evening, but Shearer did not inform her guests. "It would have spoiled my party," she reasoned.

There's No Place like Home

Newlyweds Brad Pitt and Jennifer Aniston paid $13.5 million for a six-bedroom home in Beverly Hills. The French Normandy-style mansion was built for actor Fredric March in 1933. Take a tour of some of Hollywood's most fabulous homes.

1. **DOUGLAS FAIRBANKS**

In 1920, Douglas Fairbanks bought a hunting lodge located on a hilltop on Summit Drive. The estate, located on 20 acres nearby, was intended as a gift to his fiancée, Mary Pickford. They named their home Pickfair, the first four letters of each of their last names. Pickford and Fairbanks were married there on March 28, 1920, and Pickfair became the most famous home in Hollywood. Over the years Pickford and Fairbanks hosted many parties there. Among their famous guests were Charles Lindbergh, Babe Ruth, and Henry Ford. Albert Einstein explained his theory of relativity at the dining room table using a knife, fork, and plate. Pickfair featured an oyster-shaped swimming pool and a bar that originally had been part of a Nevada saloon.

2. **JAYNE MANSFIELD**

Jayne Mansfield's house was called the Pink Palace for good reason: nearly everything in the home was painted pink. One of the Pink Palace's most distinctive features was the heart-shaped pool. The home contained 6 bedrooms and 13 bathrooms. When asked why she needed so many bathrooms, Mansfield joked that her husband and children were going to be the cleanest people in the world. She insisted she bathed in pink champagne twice a week.

3. **HAROLD LLOYD**

Harold Lloyd was one of silent films' most popular comedians. Lloyd's mansion, Greenacres, was perhaps the grandest of all the stars' homes. Built in 1927, Greenacres was a 44-room Renaissance palace in Benedict Canyon. The centerpiece of Greenacres was a 50-foot-long sunken living room with a gold-leaf coffered ceiling.

4. **MARION DAVIES**

Built in the 1930s, Marion Davies's Santa Monica beach house, known as Ocean Front, cost $7 million. It was the largest beachfront house in California, with 110 rooms. A Venetian marble bridge spanned its enormous swimming pool. The Gold Room lived up to its name: its walls were decorated in gold leaf, the draperies were covered with gold brocade, and the furniture was upholstered in gold. The house was so enormous that it was converted into a hotel in 1949.

5. **CHARLIE CHAPLIN**

When Charlie Chaplin built his 14-room house in 1922 on a 6-acre hillside site overlooking Beverly Hills, he cut costs by having his studio carpenters do much of the work. The home became known as Breakaway House because it began falling apart soon after it was completed. Chaplin spent much of his time away from the house, prompting actress Ina Claire to comment, "It isn't home, but it's much."

6. BUSTER KEATON

The other great silent film comedian, Buster Keaton, lived in an even more opulent house than Chaplin's. The Great Stone Face lived in an Italian villa-style home in Beverly Hills. Keaton threw many parties in the home, where he would dazzle guests with his incredible acrobatic entrances. He would swing down from the grand staircase like Tarzan. Keaton's career fizzled when talkies arrived, and when he divorced his wife, actress Natalie Talmadge, he was forced to move out of his mansion and live in a trailer on the MGM lot. In 1952, Keaton appeared in Charlie Chaplin's film *Limelight.* Costar Claire Bloom remembers Keaton pulling out a post-card of his fabulous home. "I lived there once," he told her wistfully. During the 1950s, the house was purchased by actor James Mason, who discovered a secret vault containing many of Keaton's rare silent film classics. The find helped to spark a revival of interest in Keaton's films.

7. RUDOLPH VALENTINO

Rudolph Valentino built his Moorish-inspired mansion, Falcon Lair, on an 8-acre piece of land overlooking Beverly Hills. Valentino's walls were covered in black leather, which contributed to the home's mysterious aura. Valentino held séances there, and it was rumored that the house was haunted by Valentino's ghost.

8. **RAMON NOVARRO**

Ramon Novarro, one of the most popular leading men of the silent film era, lived in a house designed by Frank Lloyd Wright. Famed MGM set designer Cedric Gibbons was hired to design the interiors, and Novarro insisted that his guests wear only black, white, and silver to match the black-fur-and-silver Gibbons décor.

9. **JOHN BARRYMORE**

John Barrymore's 45-room home, Bella Vista, overlooked Sunset Boulevard. The estate was composed of 16 separate buildings and featured a kidney-shaped swimming pool, a skeet-shooting range, a stocked trout pond, and an aviary that housed more than 300 exotic birds. The trophy room contained a mounted 560-pound marlin caught by Barrymore, a huge stuffed turtle, an enormous crocodile shot by Barrymore's wife, Dolores Costello, and a rare dinosaur egg. Barrymore's favorite room was a bar from Alaska that he had reassembled.

10. **AARON SPELLING**

Aaron Spelling, one of Hollywood's most successful producers, built a house to prove it. The Manor is a 65,000-square-foot palace that cost $45 million to build. Its many features include a doll museum, a 16-car garage, four bars, three kitchens, a gymnasium, theater, bowling alley, and a dozen fountains.

Car Crazy

The automobile was the ultimate status symbol of many movie stars. Mary Pickford, a close friend of Henry Ford, was given the first Model A off the assembly line. Gloria Swanson's Lancia had leopard upholstery. Rudolph Valentino's Voisin touring car had a coiled cobra radiator cap. Silent film actress Mae Murray owned two Rolls-Royces and a canary yellow Pierce-Arrow. Grace Moore boasted of having the longest automobile in Hollywood. Arnold Schwarzenegger liked his Hummer all-terrain vehicle so much he bought five more.

1. BUSTER KEATON

At one time, Buster Keaton owned 20 automobiles. His favorite was a 30-foot-long land cruiser. The schooner was actually a converted bus he had bought from the Fifth Avenue Bus Company. The vehicle had sleeping accommodations for six, two drawing rooms, a kitchen, and an observation deck. Since the car resembled a yacht, Keaton often wore an admiral's outfit while driving it.

2. SESSUE HAYAKAWA

Sessue Hayakawa was a silent film star, best remembered today for his role in the 1957 Academy Award–winning film, *The Bridge on the River Kwai.* At the height of his popularity, Hayakawa owned a gold-plated Pierce-Arrow. When he learned Fatty Arbuckle had one just like it, Hayakawa gave the car to the Long Island Fire Department.

3. FATTY ARBUCKLE

Fatty Arbuckle, who owned several automobiles, including a Rolls-Royce, a Cadillac, and a Stevens-Duryea, prided himself on owning the largest and most expensive automobiles in Hollywood. His Pierce-Arrow was equipped with a bar and a toilet.

4. CLARA BOW

Clara Bow was so proud of her red hair that she had her Kissel convertible painted flaming red. She would drive through Hollywood with her two chow dogs, which also were dyed red.

5. STEPIN FETCHIT

One of the easiest cars to recognize in Hollywood belonged to Stepin Fetchit, who owned 16 different automobiles during the 1930s. His favorite was a pink Rolls-Royce with a neon sign on the trunk that spelled out his name.

6. TOM MIX

Tom Mix was the most popular cowboy star of his time, and he played the role on and off the screen. On the hood of his car, Mix had a leather saddle and a set of steer horns. He died in an automobile accident in 1940.

7. CLARK GABLE

The rivalry between leading men Clark Gable and Gary Cooper extended to their automobiles. Gable insisted that his custom-built Duesenberg be a foot longer than Cooper's Duesenberg.

8. MARLENE DIETRICH

Marlene Dietrich owned a 1932 16-cylinder Cadillac with an extra-large trunk to accommodate her luggage. Dietrich's chauffeur wore a uniform with a mink collar and carried two revolvers.

9. FRANCIS X. BUSHMAN

Silent film star Francis X. Bushman's favorite color was lavender. He smoked lavender cigars, and his servants wore lavender uniforms, so, naturally, his car was a lavender-colored Rolls-Royce.

10. ED WOOD

Director Ed Wood was the antithesis of the Hollywood success story: he owned a beat-up black Cadillac convertible. One day a garbageman offered Wood $50 for the car. When Wood hesitated, the man offered to throw in his pet monkey. The monkey climbed onto Wood's head, where it had a bowel movement.

Clothes Encounters

Hollywood stars have their own unique fashion sense. Paulette Goddard once appeared at a party dressed in a sarong decorated with $10 bills. Frank Sinatra changed his underpants up to 10 times a day. Joan Crawford owned 16 fur coats and changed clothes as often as 10 times a day. Columbia Studio head Harry Cohn wore his monogrammed silk shirts only once before giving them away. During the Depression, actress Kay Francis suggested, in a magazine article, that women not throw away their old ermine coats, but have them cut up instead into bath mats. George Hamilton only wore his socks once. In her heyday in the 1920s, Gloria Swanson never wore the same dress twice. Yul Brynner claimed he wore black for the last 40 years of his life because it made shopping easier.

1. CHARLES BRONSON

Charles Bronson was best known for his tough guy roles in films such as *Death Wish* and *Mr. Majestyk.* Growing up in Pennsylvania in the 1920s, he was one of 15 children. His family was so poor Bronson was forced to wear his older sister's hand-me-down dresses.

2. JOAN COLLINS

Joan Collins starred in such films as *The Girl in the Red Velvet Swing* and *The Bitch,* but her role of Alexis in the television series *Dynasty* earned her the most notoriety. The glamorous star usually wore designer dresses, but at a 1982 press conference, she arrived in a dress made of newspaper clippings written about her that year.

3. JANE RUSSELL

Producer Howard Hughes was obsessed with displaying Jane Russell's cleavage in *The Outlaw.* Hughes designed a cantilevered brassiere, an early version of the push-up bra. Russell found it uncomfortable and, without telling Hughes, wore one of her own bras. Hughes never knew the difference.

4. SARAH MILES

British actress Sarah Miles starred in such films as *Blow-Up* and *Ryan's Daughter.* When her Skye terrier, Gladys, died, Miles found a way to remain close to her departed pet. She had a pair of boots made out of the dog's fur.

5. F. SCOTT FITZGERALD

In his final years as a Hollywood screenwriter, F. Scott Fitzgerald had an affair with gossip columnist Sheilah Graham. Apparently the couple was never completely nude when they had sex. Fitzgerald, who believed he had ugly feet, always wore socks, and Graham never took off her bra.

6. LILYAN TASHMAN

Lilyan Tashman, an actress popular in the early 1930s, was known as the best dressed woman in Hollywood. Her father had been a clothes manufacturer, and her fashion sense was so good she selected the wardrobe for her friend Greta Garbo. Tashman prided herself on never wearing the same outfit twice. She often greeted her guests wearing silk pajamas. For one of her parties, she asked her guests to wear only red and white. When they arrived at her house, they discovered that Tashman had painted everything in her home red and white.

7. LUPE VELEZ

Lupe Velez arrived at a Hollywood party dressed in a full-length ermine coat. She saw a chinchilla coat worn by a socialite and decided she had to have it. Velez pulled up her sleeve and revealed several expensive bracelets. She made a deal in which she traded two of her bracelets for the chinchilla coat. Velez walked back to her limousine, rolled up her ermine coat into a ball and tossed it in the trunk, and put on the chinchilla.

8. CARMEN MIRANDA

Carmen Miranda, the Brazilian bombshell, got into trouble for what she was not wearing. During a dance scene, her dress flew up above her waist, and a photographer took a picture of Miranda that revealed she was not wearing underpants. Morality groups were outraged and demanded that 20th Century-Fox not renew the actress's option.

9. GALE SONDERGAARD

For the premiere of their film *Zola,* Warner Brothers asked that their stars dress in their finest clothes. Gale Sondergaard received the most attention—she wore a black monkey fur coat and a flaming red dress.

Floyd Conner

The fashionable and flamboyant Lupe Velez.

10. **BING CROSBY**

When Bing Crosby's house caught fire in 1943, Crosby rushed to his closet to retrieve a pair of his golf shoes. The reason? Crosby had hidden $30,000 in the toes of the shoes.

It's a Gift

By the time Shirley Temple was eight years old, fans had sent her 135,000 gifts. During the filming of the 1948 film, *Daisy Kenyon,* Joan Crawford gave her costar Henry Fonda a jockstrap encrusted with diamonds and sequins. Virginia Hill, a bit player in movies and the mistress of gangster Bugsy Siegel, used to flush expensive gifts down the toilet when she was displeased with the giver. George Clooney gave girlfriend Kelly Preston a potbellied pig named Max as a birthday present. When the couple broke up, Clooney got custody of the pig. Years later, Preston's husband, John Travolta, gave her a $20 million jet as a present. One of the oddest gift exchanges involved Billy Bob Thornton and Angelina Jolie, who reportedly gave each other lockets filled with their own blood.

1. ELIZABETH TAYLOR

During her lifetime, Elizabeth Taylor has been showered with fabulous gifts by many suitors. While married to producer Michael Todd, Taylor injured her back when she slipped and fell on their yacht. To brighten up her hospital room, Todd bought paintings by Picasso, Monet, and Renoir and hung them on the walls. Husband Richard Burton bought Liz some of the world's most valuable gems, including the 33.9 carat Krupp diamond and the 69.4 carat Cartier diamond. Perhaps the strangest gift she received was from her friend Michael Jackson. The King of Pop gave her a life-size doll of himself.

2. NICOLAS CAGE

When Nicolas Cage was dating actress Patricia Arquette, she devised a treasure hunt for him to prove his love for her. Arquette gave Cage a list of three items he had to find: a black orchid, the autograph of author J. D. Salinger, and a statue from the Big Boy restaurant chain. Unable to find a black orchid, Cage dyed one that color. After trying unsuccessfully to contact the reclusive author, Cage bought an auto-graphed Salinger book for $2,500. The Big Boy statue proved to be more of a challenge. After weeks of searching, Cage brought the chubby-cheeked statue of the big boy to Arquette. Having fulfilled his quest, Cage won the heart of Arquette, and they were later married.

3. CAROLE LOMBARD

Carole Lombard was known for her outrageous sense of humor. Rather than buy husband Clark Gable an expensive automobile for Valentine's Day, she went to a junkyard and purchased a jalopy for $15. She painted red hearts all over it and presented it to him with a card that read, "You're driving me crazy." One of her more personal gifts to Gable was a hand-knitted penis warmer.

4. JOHN BARRYMORE

John Barrymore was a legendary actor who starred in the films *Twentieth Century* and *Midnight*. Barrymore was notorious for his wild lifestyle. For his 55th birthday, some of his friends gave him a nude woman wrapped in cellophane.

5. SOPHIA LOREN

What do you give to a woman who has everything? Producer Carlo Ponti presented his Oscar-winning wife, Sophia Loren, a 14-karat solid gold toilet seat.

6. MIA FARROW

Eccentric artist Salvador Dali liked to present his actress friends with unique gifts. For Mia Farrow's birthday, Dali gave her a multicolored milk bottle with a rat and mouse inside. He sent Ali MacGraw a live iguana, its tail covered with faux pearls, in a flower box.

7. RED SKELTON

Red Skelton learned that actress-dancer Ann Miller was a little nervous about going on her first airplane ride. As a going-away gift, Skelton handed Miller a beautifully wrapped present with instructions to open it once she was in the air. The present was a leather-bound scrapbook filled with newspaper clippings of airplane crashes.

8. JOAN BENNETT

Many movie stars despised gossip columnist Hedda Hopper. On Valentine's Day, actress Joan Bennett sent Hopper a skunk to show the columnist what she thought of her.

9. MARY PICKFORD

During their marriage, Mary Pickford and Douglas Fairbanks gave each other many fabulous gifts. One of the strangest was a .45 caliber pistol Pickford gave to her husband; the gun had been used to kill 20 German soldiers during combat in World War I.

10. JOHNNY WEISSMULLER

The marriage of Johnny Weissmuller and Lupe Velez was one of the most tempestuous in Hollywood. The couple had more than their share of fights, and the tiny Lupe could hold her own with her Tarzan. Velez gave Weissmuller a pair of boxing gloves with the note, "Darling, so you can punch me if I ever leave you again."

They Were What They Ate

S helley Winters once went on an ice cream diet and gained 14 pounds. Dolly Parton liked to eat cookies while watching exercise videos. Gary Cooper ate a large can of sauerkraut each morning to keep him regular. Errol Flynn brought oranges onto movie sets and injected vodka into them with hypodermic needles. Comedian Soupy Sales had more than 2,000 pies thrown in his face a year as part of his act. Actress Kelly Preston admits to a taste for Spam sandwiches. When Michael Douglas and Catherine Zeta-Jones were married in September 1999, the bride was presented with a cake in the shape of tap shoes, and the groom's cake was shaped like a golf ball. She had been a tap dancing champion, and he's an avid golfer.

1. ELVIS PRESLEY

Perhaps the star with the most unusual diet was Elvis Presley. He would hollow out a loaf of bread and fill it with peanut butter, grape jelly, and bacon. Presley loved peanut butter so much as a child in Mississippi, he hid the jar when the family had visitors. Another one of his favorite sandwiches was

peanut butter and mashed banana. One meal he loved combined crowder peas, burned bacon, mashed potatoes, and
sauerkraut, which Presley mixed together and ate with his
fingers. Presley had an enormous appetite. He occasionally
ordered as many as 100 popsicles, creamsicles, and Eskimo
pies, and, usually, all that was left was a pile of sticks. When
he went on a health food kick, he could eat 20 cups of
yogurt at one sitting. Some of Elvis's other culinary treats
included oven-fried chicken with a potato chip coating and
a 7-Up salad.

2. **HOWARD HUGHES**

Probably the only person in Hollywood with stranger taste in
food than Elvis Presley was Howard Hughes. He had very
particular and peculiar taste. During his days as owner of
RKO Studios, Hughes had the same meal every day: a steak
and 12 peas. When he was living at the Beverly Hills Hotel
during the 1950s, Hughes ordered an upside-down cake and
23 kadota figs in the middle of the night. It had to be exactly
23 figs or he would send them back. He frequently ordered
roast beef sandwiches to be left on a fork on the tree outside the window of his bungalow. Often the sandwiches
were left untouched. In his old age, Hughes became even
more eccentric. Sometimes he subsisted on Hershey's choco-
late bars with pecans.

3. **ALFRED HITCHCOCK**

Alfred Hitchcock directed *Psycho,* often considered the most
frightening movie ever made. Hitchcock had many phobias,
including a well-publicized fear of the police. His most
unusual phobia was of eggs. "I'm frightened of eggs. They
revolt me," confessed the Master of Suspense. "Have you

ever seen anything more revolting than an egg yolk breaking and spilling its yellow liquid? Blood is jolly red. But egg
yolk is yellow, revolting. I've never tasted it."

4. NASTASSJA KINSKI

Actress Nastassja Kinski, the star of a 1982 remake of *Cat
People* and *One from the Heart,* recalled a strange eating habit
she had as a child. When she was 11 years old, she used to
pluck her eyebrows, drip honey on them, and eat them as a
snack.

5. LAUREN BACALL

Once, in a New York restaurant, Lauren Bacall complained
that her baked potato was not cooked properly. She said to
the waiter, "Can't you see that this is a bad potato?" The
waiter took a closer look at the suspect spud. He reached
down and spanked the potato, saying, "Bad potato! Bad
potato!" Even Bacall had to laugh.

6. NICK NOLTE

In the 1986 film, *Down and Out in Beverly Hills,* there's a scene
in which Nick Nolte's character showed a dog how to eat out
of a bowl. To make the scene more realistic, Nolte actually
ate real dog food.

7. ALICIA SILVERSTONE

Alicia Silverstone, delightful as a rich girl in *Clueless,* has
some distinctive tastes in food. Her two favorite cereals are
Lucky Charms and Cocoa Puffs, but her most unusual crav-
ing is for apricot baby food.

8. **CHER**

Dancer Marc Connally said that Cher once put strawberries and cream on her body. As part of their sexual foreplay, the Oscar-winning actress fed Connally with strawberries and cream from her body.

9. **BRUCE LEE**

Martial arts film star Bruce Lee was known for his excellent conditioning. He credited his magnificent physique to his diet of raw beef, eggs, and a glass of beef blood.

10. **JAMES CAGNEY**

James Cagney played a gangster in the 1931 film classic, *The Public Enemy.* In the film's most famous scene, Cagney smashes a grapefruit half into Mae Clarke's face. That scene came back to haunt Cagney; whenever he would go to a restaurant, diners would send over a complimentary grapefruit. It got to be so bad Cagney stopped going to restaurants.

Pampered Pets

At the age of 12, Elizabeth Taylor wrote a children's book, entitled *Nibbles and Me,* about her pet chipmunk. Francis X. Bushman had more than 300 Great Danes on his estate. Lilyan Tashman served her pet cat high tea each afternoon. Brigitte Nielsen had braces put on her poodle puppy's teeth. Madonna presented her pet Chihuahua, Chiquita, with a $7,500 diamond choker from Tiffany.

1. JOHN BARRYMORE

John Barrymore named his Kerry blue terriers Shake, Quake, and Shock because they were born during an earthquake. Barrymore fed his pet vulture, Mahoney, rotten meat he found in his neighbor's garbage cans. Barrymore taught Mahoney to sit on his shoulder and preen his mustache, after which the actor would reward the bird with a kiss on the beak.

2. JOAN CRAWFORD

Joan Crawford's pet poodle, Cliquot, received treatment most people would envy. He was fed sirloin steak, chicken breast, and ice cream, and he wore costumes color-coordinated with his master's clothing. Crawford ordered Cliquot's tailored jackets and velvet collars from Hammacher Schlemmer. He even had his own tiny facial tissues in case of a runny nose.

3. **EMIL JANNINGS**

Emil Jannings won the first-ever Academy Award for Best Actor in 1928. At his home on Hollywood Boulevard, Jannings kept a chicken coop, whose denizens were named after other actors: Rudolph Valentino, Greta Garbo, John Gilbert, Pola Negri, and Conrad Veidt, among others.

4. **AVA GARDNER**

Ava Gardner was one of the most beautiful actresses ever to appear in the movies. Two of her best performances came in *Mogambo* and *The Barefoot Contessa.* When Gardner died in 1990, her will included a monthly allowance for her dog, Morgan. The dog also had its own maid and chauffeur.

5. **ESTELLE TAYLOR**

Estelle Taylor was a popular actress of the 1920s who was married to heavyweight boxing champion Jack Dempsey. Taylor owned a 300-pound blue hoarhound named Castor. The monstrous dog could have played the Hound of the Baskervilles. Taylor took Castor on a trip to Paris where he trashed a hotel room, causing $10,000 in damage. He also mauled an Airedale to death and broke the arm of his handler.

6. **LIBERACE**

Liberace appeared as a casket salesman in the 1965 film comedy *The Loved One.* The flamboyant pianist's trademark was his outrageous clothing. He even treated his pet poodle with extravagance, dining with him and even giving him his own chair.

7. LUPE VELEZ

Lupe Velez had 75 pet canaries, and she knew every one of them by name. She also kept two golden eagles, a gift from her lover, Gary Cooper, in a huge cage in her backyard.

8. ELIZABETH TAYLOR

Elizabeth Taylor's star-making role was in the 1944 film, *National Velvet.* The movie told the story of a young girl who rides her horse in the Grand National horse race. Taylor loved the horse so much she asked for him as her 13th birthday present. The studio gave Taylor the horse. Fifteen years later, producer Pandro Berman, who gave the horse to Taylor, ran into the star and got an unexpected reception. Taylor's affection for the horse had long since waned, and she was upset because she was still paying for the horse's feed and stable costs.

9. JAMES DEAN

During the filming of *Giant,* Elizabeth Taylor gave costar James Dean a Siamese cat named Marcus. One day, Dean showed up at the door of his friend Jeanette Mille. He handed her the kitten and left without saying a word. The next day, the actor was killed in an automobile accident.

10. BUSTER KEATON

Buster Keaton's dog, Trotsky, had an unusual way of sleeping. The Irish wolfhound slept submerged in the swimming pool, with only its head out of the water.

Amazing Animal Actors

Some animal actors have become bigger stars than their human costars. A collie named Lassie starred in several films and had her own television program. Fury, Champion, and Silver were equine actors with star power. From *Flicka* to *Francis the Talking Mule,* animals have been some of the most popular actors in Hollywood.

1. RIN TIN TIN

Rin Tin Tin appeared in his first film, *Where the North Begins,* in 1923. The German shepherd was so popular he helped save Warner Brothers from bankruptcy. Studio executive Darryl F. Zanuck actually wrote scripts for the dog's movies. Rin Tin Tin had his own valet, limousine, and five-room dressing room. At the peak of his popularity, the dog received 2,000 fan letters a day. The original Rin Tin Tin died in 1932; other dogs continued to play the role, and Rin Tin Tin had his own television program from 1954 to 1959.

2. TRIGGER

Trigger was a golden palomino that appeared in 80 Roy Rogers westerns and on the cowboy star's television program, which aired from 1951 to 1957. Trigger, whose real name was Golden Cloud, had appeared as Maid Marian's horse in the 1938 film *The Adventures of Robin Hood*. Roy Rogers, who was only making $75 a week, paid $2,500 for the horse on an installment plan. The intelligent horse was able to perform more than 60 tricks, and, a star in his own right, Trigger had his hoofprints preserved in cement in front of Grauman's Chinese Theater in 1949.

When Trigger died in 1965, Rogers had the horse mounted, and he became an attraction in the Roy Rogers and Dale Evans Museum in Victorville, California. Buttermilk, Dale Evans's horse, and Bullet the Wonder Dog were stuffed and put on display in the museum as well. Rogers joked, "When my time comes, just skin me and put me right up there on Trigger." Fans of taxidermy were disappointed when Rogers passed away and was not put on display in his museum.

3. **J. FRED MUGGS**

J. Fred Muggs was a chimpanzee who appeared on *The Today Show* from 1953 to 1957. The well-dressed chimp, who had 450 outfits, was also an artist who did more than 10,000 finger paintings.

4. **GENTLE BEN**

Gentle Ben was a 650-pound black bear who starred in his own television show from 1967 to 1969. His daily diet consisted of five loaves of bread, a half-dozen apples and oranges, and bunches of carrots. Occasionally he ate candy, doughnuts, and lemon drops and drank soft drinks. Trainers tried pouring Chanel No. 5 on his food to curtail his appetite, but to no avail.

5. **TOTO**

Toto was the cairn terrier who was Dorothy's pet in *The Wizard of Oz*. The small dog, whose real name was Terry, was blown over repeatedly by the wind machines used to simulate the tornado, so a stuffed animal was used as a stand-in. Toto was forced to miss several weeks of shooting when one of the Wicked Witch's guards accidentally stepped on his paw.

6. **FRED**

Fred the cockatoo appeared in the television program *Baretta,* which aired from 1975 to 1978. The bird was so popular he received more fan mail than the program's star, Robert Blake. The bird was very intelligent and was afraid Blake would drop him. He would say, "Don't hurt Fred," even though no one had taught him to. Another time, he chased Blake around the room, pecking at him mercilessly.

7. **BONZO**

Bonzo was the chimp who co-starred with Ronald Reagan in the 1951 film, *Bedtime for Bonzo*. Reagan played a professor who, as part of an experiment, treated a chimpanzee as a child. During one scene, Bonzo grabbed Reagan's tie and nearly choked the future President before Bonzo's trainer was able to loosen the knot.

8. **CLARENCE**

Clarence the Cross-Eyed Lion starred in his own movie in 1965 and in the television program *Daktari,* from 1966 to 1969. The lion's vision was so bad that a special pair of glasses was made to correct his vision. The overly docile Clarence had to have a stand-in lion to roar for him.

9. BABE

Babe, the 1995 film about a talking pig, garnered seven Oscar nominations. In reality, 48 different pigs played the role of Babe; makeup artists put black toupees on the pigs to make them look alike.

10. MISTER ED

Mister Ed was a television sitcom about a talking horse and aired from 1961 to 1966. Mister Ed, whose real name was Bamboo Harvester, drank a gallon of tea each day. The voice of Mister Ed was spoken by cowboy star Rocky Lane.

Stage Mothers

Natalie Wood's mother reportedly tore off a butterfly's wings to make her daughter cry for a movie scene. The mother of actress Veronica Lake sued her for nonsupport. For better or worse, mothers often play leading roles in the careers of their children.

1. CLARA BOW

Clara Bow's mother, Sarah, was the antithesis of the typical stage mother: she threatened to kill her daughter if she went to Hollywood. One night Clara woke up to her mother holding a butcher knife to her throat. Sarah was committed to a mental hospital, and Clara became a star. She never got over the traumatic experience and suffered from insomnia for the rest of her life.

2. JEAN HARLOW

In June 1937, Jean Harlow fell ill with a life-threatening illness. Although it became apparent that her daughter was extremely ill, Mama Jean refused to call a doctor because she was a Christian Scientist. By the time Jean's friends were able to get her to a hospital, it was too late. She died of uremic poisoning on June 7, 1937, at the age of 26. If she had received prompt medical attention, it is likely Harlow would have survived.

3. FRANCES FARMER

Beautiful and talented Frances Farmer was one of the most promising actresses of the 1930s. Frances's rebellious nature resulted in problems with the studio and run-ins with the law. In 1944, Frances's mother, Lillian, agreed to commit her daughter to The Western Washington State Hospital. Even though Farmer was released eventually, her career as an actress was over.

4. GARY COOPER

During the 1930s, Gary Cooper was one of the most eligible bachelors in Hollywood. Cooper dated many women, none of whom met with his mother's approval. Alice Cooper, a proper Englishwoman, always managed to find fault with his dates. Alice so disapproved of his romance with Lupe Velez it was rumored that she threatened to kill herself if they married.

5. RUSS COLUMBO

Singer-turned-actor Russ Columbo was killed in an accidental shooting in 1934. His mother, Julia, who was recovering from a heart attack, was never told of her son's death. She was told her son was on a prolonged world tour, and the family fabricated letters from Russ. When Julia died 10 years later, her last words were instructions to tell Russ how proud he had made her. She even left part of her estate to her long-dead son.

6. CLIFTON WEBB

Character actor Clifton Webb rarely made a major decision without consulting his mother, Maybelle. She was over 90 years old when she died in 1960. Webb was so distraught Noel Coward said, "It must be terrible to be orphaned at 71."

7. MARY PICKFORD

The personification of the stage mother was Mary Pickford's mother, Charlotte. She advised Mary on every aspect of her career, from acting to financial matters. With her mother's help, Pickford became the highest-paid film actress of her day. At her peak, Mary Pickford was paid $250,000 a picture, and her mother was paid $50,000.

8. BROOKE SHIELDS

Brooke Shields was only five days old when her mother, Terri, decided that Brooke was going to have a career in show business: "She was the most beautiful thing that I'd ever seen in my life, and ... her beauty was going to contribute to mankind." Terri helped make Brooke into a child star, but some of her decisions were questionable. Brooke posed nude for the first time at age eight, and two years later, she was paid $45 to appear in *Playboy*. In 1978, she played a child prostitute in the film *Pretty Baby*. Despite the nudity, Shields was able to maintain her wholesome image.

9. SHIRLEY TEMPLE

Shirley Temple's mother, Gertrude, was always on the set during her films. She would stand outside of the camera range, whispering to her daughter, "Sparkle! Shirley,

Sparkle!" Temple became the most popular child star in motion picture history.

10. **MARY ASTOR**

Mary Astor was 15 years old when she made her film debut in 1921. Thirteen years later, her parents sued her for non-support, claiming they needed more money to renovate the home their daughter had bought for them.

Faces to Die For

Some of the most beautiful women in the world have been film actresses. With her violet eyes, Elizabeth Taylor was often described as the most beautiful woman in the world. Audrey Hepburn had an almost childlike beauty. Catherine Deneuve had a flawless face. Julia Roberts personified the modern pretty woman. Don't hate them because they're beautiful.

1. NASTASSJA KINSKI

The daughter of actor Klaus Kinski, Nastassja Kinski rose to stardom as the tragic title character in Roman Polanski's *Tess*. In the early 1980s, her face seemed to be on every magazine cover, even *Time*. John Simon, the most acerbic of critics, wrote a glowing cover story about her in *Rolling Stone*, and a nude poster of her entwined with a boa constrictor became a best seller. Although she starred in films made by directors such as Frances Ford Coppola, Roman Polanski, and Hugh Hudson, her films often did poorly at the box office.

2. LOUISE BROOKS

Film historian Henri Langlois said in the 1950s, "There is no Garbo! There is no Dietrich! There is only Louise Brooks." Brooks was a star in Hollywood in the late 1920s, but her reputation today is based on two films made in Germany with director G. W. Pabst, *Pandora's Box* and *Diary of a Lost Girl*. Unlike most silent film stars, Brooks's natural acting style does not appear dated. A tremendous beauty, Brooks was known for her trademark black bob hairstyle. Critic Kenneth Tynan wrote a memorable homage to Brooks that was published in *The New Yorker*.

3. JORDANA BREWSTER

One of the most beautiful young actresses is Brazilian-born Jordana Brewster. Her mother, Maria, was a model who was featured in the *Sports Illustrated* swimsuit edition. Rob Cohen, Brewster's director in the hit film, *The Fast and the Furious,* called her, "one of the most beautiful women on the screen." Her costar, Paul Walker, summed it up best when he said, "She's a knockout."

4. RACHEL WARD

Rachel Ward was so beautiful her limited acting range almost went unnoticed. The tall British brunette became a star in 1980 with her performance as a high-priced call girl in *Sharky's Machine,* but her biggest success was in the film *Against All Odds.* She also played Richard Chamberlain's star-crossed lover in the enormously popular television miniseries, *The Thorn Birds.* In recent years, Ward has appeared in a number of made-for-television films.

5. **PAULINA PORIZKOVA**

Many models have attempted careers as movie actresses, and none was as beautiful as Paulina Porizkova. The Czech supermodel debuted as—what else?—a Czech supermodel, in *Anna.* She also co-starred with Tom Selleck in *Her Alibi.* Porizkova now stars in mostly small, independent features and is married to rock star Ric Ocasek.

6. **HALLE BERRY**

It's not surprising that Halle Berry won a number of beauty contests before becoming an actress. Drop-dead gorgeous, Berry starred in numerous films in the 1990s, including *Jungle Fever* and *Bulworth.* She ended the decade with her critically acclaimed portrayal of Dorothy Dandridge in a made-for-television film, *Introducing Dorothy Dandridge,* for which she won an Emmy. Berry did a topless scene in the film *Swordfish,* then displayed her considerable acting talent in her Oscar-winning performance in *Monster's Ball.*

7. **PENÉLOPE CRUZ**

Spanish-born beauty Penélope Cruz was only 18 when she starred in *Belle Epoque* in 1992. Eight years later, she had her American breakthrough in *Blow,* with Johnny Depp. Her romance with Tom Cruise, her costar in *Vanilla Sky,* led to speculation that she would become Penélope Cruz Cruise.

8. **DOLORES DEL RIO**

Mexican actress Dolores Del Rio is better remembered for her beauty than for her many film roles. Orson Welles, who had a highly publicized affair with Del Rio, said, "I thought

Photofest

Penélope Cruz in *Blow* (2001).

she was the most beautiful woman I'd ever seen." Director John Ford remarked, "As a beauty, Dolores is in a class with Garbo." German novelist Erich Maria Remarque said of Del Rio, "Every part of her was beautiful."

9. GRETA GARBO

For many, Greta Garbo personified screen beauty and glamour. Robert Sherwood, *Life* magazine's film critic, referred to her as the "Dream Princess." Costar and lover John Gilbert called Garbo, "The most alluring creature I've ever seen." According to director Mauritz Stiller, "You get a face like that in front of a camera only once in a lifetime." Writer Kenneth Tynan summed up the feeling of her admirers when he wrote, "What when drunk one sees in other women, one sees in Garbo sober."

10. HEDY LAMARR

Born Hedwig Kiesler, Hedy Lamarr took her screen name from the silent film actress, Barbara La Marr, who was nicknamed, "Too Beautiful." Louis B. Mayer called Hedy Lamarr, "the most beautiful girl in the world." George Sanders said she was so beautiful that, whenever she walked into a room, everyone stopped talking and stared at her. According to Sanders, when she spoke, "I just watched her mouth moving and marveled at the exquisite shapes made by her lips. I didn't hear a word she said."

Sex Symbols

Ever since Theda Bara became the first vamp, Hollywood has given us many screen goddesses. Lana Turner was the original sweater girl. Buxom brunette Jane Russell proved that blondes weren't the only ones having fun. In the 1960s, Ann-Margret became the screen's most popular sex kitten. Pamela Anderson, *Playboy* centerfold and *Baywatch* beauty, was the reigning sex symbol of the 1990s. Voluptuous Italian beauty Monica Bellucci, star of *Malena* and *The Brotherhood of the Wolves*, is the latest foreign sex goddess.

1. MARILYN MONROE

Universally considered the number one screen sex symbol, Marilyn Monroe has become a popular culture icon. According to actress Cybill Shepherd, Monroe "had curves in places where other people don't even have places." When asked what she wore to bed, Marilyn replied, "Chanel No. 5." Also a talented screen comedienne, Monroe was memorable in *How to Marry a Millionaire, The Seven Year Itch,* and *Some Like It Hot.* Who can forget the scene in *The Seven Year Itch* where

Monroe stands on a subway grate, her dress billowing up to her waist?

2. ELIZABETH TAYLOR

Elizabeth Taylor was one of the most beautiful movie stars and one of the sexiest. Husband Richard Burton said her breasts could "topple empires." Her cleavage was on display in many of her films, such as *The VIPs, Doctor Faustus,* and *The Taming of the Shrew.* When Taylor emerges from the water dressed in a nearly transparent white swimsuit at the end of *Suddenly Last Summer,* it is one of film's sexiest moments. During the filming of *The Last Time I Saw Paris,* MGM hired a "bust inspector." The prim woman with wire-rimmed glasses climbed atop a ladder to look down at Taylor's dress to make sure not too much cleavage was exposed. Director Richard Brooks screamed at the woman, who fled the set in tears.

3. JAYNE MANSFIELD

The ultimate blonde bombshell, Jayne Mansfield measured a spectacular 40(D)-21-35. Mansfield's movie career paled in comparison with that of Hollywood's other major blonde sex symbol, Marilyn Monroe, but no one could deny her sex appeal. Many of her films bordered on self-parody. Viewers got the point in the film *The Girl Can't Help It,* when Mansfield held up a pair of milk bottles in front of her enormous breasts.

4. RITA HAYWORTH

Rita Hayworth was known as the "Love Goddess." On the cover of the August 11, 1941, issue of *Life* magazine, Hayworth, clad in a black silk and satin nightgown, posed kneeling on a bed. When Orson Welles saw the sexy photo, he vowed to marry Hayworth, whom he had never met; a few years later he did. Hayworth was considered such a bombshell her image was put on the atomic bombs dropped on Bikini atoll.

5. BRIGITTE BARDOT

Blonde French actress Brigitte Bardot created a sensation with her sultry performance in the 1957 film *And God Created Woman.* Bardot's sex kitten image helped to introduce a greater sensuality to film.

6. SOPHIA LOREN

Sophia Loren, Gina Lollobrigida, and Claudia Cardinale were the three great film sex symbols from Italy. Loren was not only an earthy sex goddess, she was an accomplished actress who won an Academy Award for her performance in the 1961 film *Two Women.* When Alan Ladd co-starred with Loren in the film *Boy on a Dolphin,* he described his love scenes with the busty Loren as being "bombed by watermelons." Loren defined sex appeal as "50 percent what you've got and 50 percent what people *think* you've got."

7. RAQUEL WELCH

At the 1969 Academy Awards, Raquel Welch presented the award for Special Visual Effects. "These are two of them," she said, obviously referring to her breasts. Welch displayed her assets in films such as *One Hundred Years B.C.* and *Fathom.* She also co-starred with Bill Cosby in the 1976 film *Mother, Jugs, and Speed.* Welch played Jugs.

8. **JEAN HARLOW**

The first great movie sex symbol, platinum blonde Jean Harlow emerged as a star in the 1930 film *Hell's Angels.* During the early 1930s, she became one of Hollywood's most popular stars, in films such as *Dinner at Eight* and *Bombshell.* Her untimely death in 1937, at the age of 26, deprived film of one of its most vibrant talents.

9. **CLARA BOW**

Clara Bow was known as the "It Girl." "It" was a sensual force, and Bow certainly had it. She received up to 30,000 fan letters a month, many of them marriage proposals from lovesick fans. The actress with the flaming red hair defined sex appeal in the Jazz Age, but Bow's lifestyle caused her to burn out quickly. "Being a sex symbol is a heavy load to carry," she lamented, "especially when one is very tired, hurt, and bewildered." According to Bow, "The more I see of men, the more I like dogs."

10. **HARRIET ANDERSSON**

In the 1950s and '60s, Harriet Andersson brought sex appeal to the films of the great Swedish director, Ingmar Bergman, who recalled, "We were all crazy about her." Andersson's natural sensuality is evident in such films as *Monika* and *Smiles of a Summer Night.* Film critic Pauline Kael wrote that one of Andersson's scenes in *The Naked Night* left the audiences "slightly out of breath."

In Like Flynn

Hollywood has had its share of ladies' men: Steve McQueen, Ryan O'Neal, and Woody Harrelson are just a few of the actors with reputations as lady killers.

1. WARREN BEATTY

Warren Beatty is an accomplished actor, director, and producer, but he will always be known as the ultimate Hollywood ladies' man. Woody Allen joked that if he came back in another life, he would like to be Warren Beatty's fingertips. According to Beatty's sister, Shirley MacLaine, "Sex is the most important thing in his life." Britt Ekland called Beatty "the most divine lover of all," and said, "I have never experienced such pleasure and passion." Another lover, Joan Collins, marveled at his sexual prowess: "He was insatiable. Three, four, five times a day was not unusual for him." Sonia Braga asked, "Who in Hollywood hasn't made love with him?" A partial list of Beatty's romantic interests includes Julie Christie, Natalie Wood, Madonna, Leslie Caron, Diane Keaton, Michelle Phillips, and Carly Simon. The seemingly confirmed bachelor married his *Bugsy* costar, Annette Bening, in 1992.

2. ERROL FLYNN

Incredibly handsome Errol Flynn estimated he had 14,000 sexual encounters during his life. The self-proclaimed phallic symbol of the world, Flynn said he didn't have to seduce girls because they were already hiding under his bed when he came home. His custom-built Packard had push-button reclining seats for lovemaking. He became so notorious for his womanizing the term "in like Flynn" came to signify ease with sexual relations. Flynn claimed he placed cocaine on the tip of his penis to heighten sexual pleasure.

3. GARY COOPER

According to Ingrid Bergman, "Every woman who knew him fell in love with Gary Cooper." Director Stuart Heisler called him "the greatest cocksman who ever lived." Clara Bow said of her lover, "He was hung like a horse and could go all night." Director Howard Hawks described Cooper's favorite method of seduction: "If I ever saw him with a good-looking girl and he'd kind of be dragging his feet over the ground and being very shy and looking down, I'd say, 'Uh-oh, the snake's going to strike again.' He found the little bashful boy approach was very successful."

4. WILT CHAMBERLAIN

Wilt Chamberlain was a Hall of Fame basketball player who once scored 100 points in an NBA game. Following his retirement from basketball, Chamberlain became an actor and co-starred with Arnold Schwarzenegger in the film *Conan the Destroyer*. Chamberlain revealed that he had more than 20,000 lovers in his life. "Actually, if you look at it, you can say that I had so many women because I was such a bad lover that they never came back a second time," Chamberlain joked.

5. JOHN BARRYMORE

John Barrymore was called The Great Lover with good reason. "I've had every woman I ever wanted," he boasted. His sexual appetite was enormous. Barrymore once rented an entire brothel in Madras, India, for a week, where, he claimed, he tried 39 sexual positions from the *Kama Sutra.*

6. CLARK GABLE

Clark Gable was once shown a publicity photograph that pictured all of MGM's leading actresses. Gable proudly proclaimed, "What wonderful display of beautiful women, and I've had every one of them." Although Gable had no trouble bedding women, he admitted he was not the greatest lover in the world. The King confessed, "As many a disappointed young lady will tell you, I'm a lousy lover."

7. GEORGE RAFT

Tough guy George Raft appeared in many films, most notably *Scarface* and *Some Like It Hot.* Known as a prolific lover, Raft allegedly averaged two lovers per day. On one occasion, he had sex with seven chorus girls in one night.

8. PORFIRIO RUBIROSA

Porfirio Rubirosa was not an actor, but he was as well known in Hollywood as most stars. Rubirosa had romances with many actresses, including Zsa Zsa Gabor and Ava Gardner. The Dominican playboy had a legendary reputation as a lover. It was said that his penis was nearly a foot long and as thick as a beer can.

9. **JAMES STEWART**

Jimmy Stewart may have seemed to be an unlikely ladies' man, but he was very popular in his bachelor days. By one count, Stewart dated more than 250 different actresses before marrying at age 41. His marriage turned out to be one of Hollywood's happiest.

10. **CHARLIE SHEEN**

Charlie Sheen was rumored to be a client of Heidi Fleiss's high-priced call girl service. It was said that Sheen was turned on by women dressed as cheerleaders. Shortly after the scandal broke, Jay Leno filmed a comic bit on *The Tonight Show* in which he sent a camera crew to Sheen's house. While Sheen denied he had a cheerleader fixation, several women dressed as cheerleaders cavorted in the background.

Kiss and Tell

Laurence Harvey said that kissing costar Capucine during the filming of *Walk on the Wild Side* was like "kissing the side of a beer bottle." According to Marilyn Monroe, "Hollywood is a place where they'll pay you $50,000 for a kiss and 50 cents for your soul." Alice Faye claimed that kissing Tyrone Power was like dying and going to heaven. At the other extreme, Kirsten Dunst complained that kissing Brad Pitt in *Interview with the Vampire* was "horrible." Silent film actor Lou Tellegen was the model for Rodin's famous sculpture, "The Kiss." When someone caught Chico Marx kissing a chorus girl, he said, "I wasn't kissing her, I was whispering in her mouth." Here are some Hollywood kisses to remember.

1. JOHN BARRYMORE

The record for kisses in a film was 191 in the 1926 film, *Don Juan*. The legendary lover was played by John Barrymore, and receiving most of his kisses were Mary Astor and Estelle Taylor.

2. REGIS TOOMEY AND JANE WYMAN

The longest kiss in screen history occurred in the 1941 film *You're in the Army*. Regis Toomey and Jane Wyman puckered up for three minutes and five seconds. At the time, Wyman, an Oscar-winning actress, was the first wife of Ronald Reagan.

3. MARY PICKFORD

Russian Sergei Komorov directed the film *The Kiss of Mary Pickford*. Amazingly, the film was made without the knowledge of its star, Mary Pickford. Komorov posed as a newsreel photographer covering Pickford's July 1926 visit to Moscow. Instead, Komorov was filming a comedy about a film extra who was determined to kiss America's sweetheart. To this day, no one knows how he was able to film the shot where Pickford kissed him.

4. CLARA BOW

Clara Bow had a number of passionate affairs during the 1920s, including a romance with Yale football star Robert Savage. Savage admitted that Bow kissed him so hard his lips bled for days.

5. ANTHONY QUINN

The 1960 murder mystery *Portrait in Black* starred Anthony Quinn and Lana Turner. During one scene, Quinn broke one of Turner's teeth by kissing her so hard.

6. JANE FONDA AND WARREN BEATTY

Jane Fonda and Warren Beatty were just beginning their movie careers when they did a screen test for the 1961 film

Parrish. Fonda remembered, "We kissed until we had practically eaten each other's heads off."

7. JOHN RICE AND MAY IRWIN

The first screen kiss took place in the 1896 film, *The Widow Jones,* starring John Rice and May Irwin. Racy for its day, the kiss outraged some critics. One review contained just two words: "Absolutely disgusting."

8. MARLENE DIETRICH

During World War II, The Hollywood Canteen, located on Cahuenga Boulevard, was a haven for servicemen. Many actresses, including Joan Crawford, Ingrid Bergman, Rita Hayworth, Hedy Lamarr, Dorothy Lamour, and Betty Grable, danced with GIs. Carl Bell, a sergeant from Texas, was allowed to kiss Marlene Dietrich because he was the millionth soldier to walk through the door of the Canteen.

9. TONY CURTIS

Most men would have loved to have kissed Marilyn Monroe; Tony Curtis was the exception. Curtis, Monroe's costar in *Some Like It Hot,* said kissing Monroe was "like kissing Hitler."

10. EVELYN VENABLE

When young actress Evelyn Venable signed a contract with Paramount, her protective father insisted on including a clause in her contract that precluded the actress from being kissed on screen. The no-kiss clause may have hampered her career; she never became a star.

Deflowered

In Hollywood, flowers have been used to express many different sentiments. Director Blake Edwards said actress Julie Andrews was "so sweet that she probably had violets between her legs." Andrews heard about the remark and sent Edwards a bouquet of violets. It marked the beginning of a romance, and they eventually married.

1. HOWARD HUGHES

Howard Hughes often used flowers in his pursuit of actresses. Once, while flying his plane, he showered flower petals on Billie Dove, who was riding on horseback below. He sent Olivia de Havilland 13 white orchids each week. Hughes became Bette Davis's lover while the actress was still married to bandleader Ham Nelson. Nelson learned of the romance and demanded that Hughes pay him $70,000 or he would make the affair public. At the time, such a scandal might have destroyed Davis's career. Hughes paid the ransom, but Davis insisted on repaying Hughes. Although Hughes was one of the wealthiest men in the country, he accepted the money. The romance between Hughes and Davis soon cooled. One year later, to commemorate the repayment, Hughes sent

Davis a single flower, the most expensive one she would ever receive.

2. OLEG CASSINI

Designer Oleg Cassini conceived an ingenious plan to win Grace Kelly's favor. Each day for 10 days, he sent a dozen red roses to her Manhattan townhouse with a card that read, "The Friendly Florist." On the 10th day, he delivered the roses himself and introduced himself as the Friendly Florist. They soon began dating.

3. CLARK GABLE

During a break in shooting *Gone With the Wind,* Clark Gable decided to marry longtime love Carole Lombard. They hopped into a blue DeSoto and drove 400 miles to Kingman, Arizona. Lombard insisted on having flowers for the wedding, so they stopped at a floral shop on the way. Gable peeled off a dollar bill and asked Lombard to bring back change. She returned with two carnation boutonnieres, a corsage of lilies of the valley and pink roses, and 50 cents in change.

4. DOLORES DEL RIO

Columnist Fred Othman wrote that Dolores Del Rio ate orchid omelets. Del Rio invited Othman to her house for lunch and served him a silver platter full of gardenias. Othman did not ask for seconds.

5. LAUREN HOLLY

On Valentine's Day, actress Lauren Holly planned a special surprise for her then-boyfriend, Jim Carrey. A note on the door instructed Carrey to follow the path of rose petals, which led him to a bath of milk and honey. The sexy actress greeted him in a skimpy white nightgown.

6. JOE DIMAGGIO

Marilyn Monroe was married to baseball legend Joe DiMaggio in 1954. Although the marriage lasted only nine months, Joe and Marilyn remained close until her death in 1962. For 20 years after Monroe's death, DiMaggio had red roses delivered to her grave three times a week.

7. ZSA ZSA GABOR

Shoe tycoon Harry Karl bought Zsa Zsa Gabor many expensive gifts during their romance. When Zsa Zsa performed at the Riviera in Las Vegas, he sent her $30,000 worth of purple orchids.

8. GRETA GARBO

Greta Garbo gave Cecil Beaton a yellow rose at their first meeting. Beaton preserved the keepsake in a notebook, and, after his death, the rose was sold for $1,000.

9. GIG YOUNG

When Gig Young won an Academy Award for Best Supporting Actor in 1969 for his performance in *They Shoot Horses, Don't They?*, he received a flower basket from Elizabeth Taylor and Richard Burton. Young was perplexed by the gift, which was accompanied by a card that read, "from Elizabeth and Richard." "I don't know any Elizabeth and Richard," he said, "Why don't people sign their names?"

10. GWYNETH PALTROW

Gwyneth Paltrow won an Oscar for Best Actress for her performance in *Shakespeare in Love.* Paltrow recalled a Valentine's Day when she was expecting a bouquet of flowers from her boyfriend. She received a huge bouquet of roses, only to discover they were from her father. An hour later, another bouquet of roses arrived, this time from her grandfather. Shortly thereafter, a third bouquet of flowers was delivered. Paltrow eagerly read the gift card only to discover they came from an ex-boyfriend she no longer liked. The roses from her new beau never arrived. The next day he told her he had sent flowers, but they had not been delivered.

Sleeping with the Stars

The bedroom is the most personal room in the home, usually reflecting the taste of its owner. Movie stars' beds come in all shapes and sizes.

1. SARAH BERNHARDT

Sarah Bernhardt was the most acclaimed stage actress of her time. Near the end of her life, The Divine Sarah starred in such silent films as the 1912 epic, *Queen Elizabeth*. Bernhardt had the unusual habit of sleeping in a satin-lined rosewood coffin. She had suffered from tuberculosis and was not expected to live, so her family bought the coffin. Bernhardt survived the deadly illness, but she kept the coffin, sleeping in it occasionally and even using it for sexual trysts. She claimed to have had 1,000 lovers during her life. When Bernhardt died in 1923, the coffin was finally put to its intended use.

2. MAE WEST

Mae West said she did her best work in bed; she entertained her lovers in a golden shell bed. One of her sexual marathons lasted 15 hours, and West even conducted interviews while lying on the bed.

3. ERROL FLYNN

Errol Flynn's home on Mulholland Drive was filled with sexual surprises. On the wall of the first-floor den, behind the fish tank, was a mural of fish with huge testicles. To open the cocktail cabinet, the bartender had to press a handle in the form of bull testicles. When the cushion of a trick chair was pressed, an artificial penis arose. Flynn's bed was covered in Russian sable, and black silk drapes covered with golden question marks surrounded the bed.

4. JOSEPHINE BAKER

Dancer Josephine Baker was the first African-American to star at the Folies Bergère. Baker caused a sensation in Europe with her provocative dances and revealing outfits: she danced nude except for a band of feathers around her waist or a belt made out of bananas. Baker starred in a series of films in France. Among her many lovers, one experience stood out. In 1929, Crown Prince Adolf of Sweden invited Baker to visit his summer palace. The future king transported her to his private railroad car with its solid gold interior, where Baker was escorted to the sleeping car that had a fantastic swan-shaped bed covered with satin sheets. The prince placed a diamond bracelet on Josephine's wrist, and the two made passionate love to the rhythm of the moving train.

5. ANN-MARGRET

In 1966, when Elvis Presley co-starred with Ann-Margret in *Viva Las Vegas,* a romance developed offscreen. One of the presents Elvis gave Ann-Margret was an enormous custom-built round pink bed.

6. ELVIS PRESLEY

Elvis Presley's taste sometimes bordered on the garish. His bed was a double king size with a black Naugahyde headboard.

7. JAYNE MANSFIELD

Almost everything in Jayne Mansfield's home was pink and heart-shaped, including the crib, bathtub, and swimming pool. The centerpiece of the house was a large heart-shaped bed on which Mansfield frequently posed for publicity photos.

8. JEAN HARLOW

Jean Harlow's bed was a replica of the scallop shell in the famous Botticelli painting "The Birth of Venus." Venus was the Roman goddess of love, and Harlow was one of the silver screen's first love goddesses.

9. PETER SELLERS

British comedian Peter Sellers, who received Academy Award nominations for his performances in *Dr. Strangelove* and *Being There,* had an unusual sleeping habit. He could sleep only if his bed was in an east-west position.

10. LUPE VELEZ

Lupe Velez's bedroom featured a polar bear skin rug, mirrored walls, white satin drapes, and statues of the Madonna and saints. She was especially proud of her eight-foot bed with its rainbow-shaped headboard, covered with gold, silver, and black lacquer. When Velez committed suicide, her oversize bed went for only $45 at the estate auction.

Odd Couples

Many were surprised when actress Julia Roberts married wild-haired country singer Lyle Lovett. Like so many marriages in Hollywood, the union was short-lived; these relationships were not meant to last.

1. SONJA HENIE AND LIBERACE

Sonja Henie, the three-time figure skating gold medalist-turned-movie star, met the flamboyant pianist Liberace at Ciro's in Hollywood. She sent him a pair of ice sculptures, one of her skating and the other of him at the piano, and they spent romantic evenings at her Bel Air mansion watching her movies. Henie announced they planned to be married, but the wedding never took place.

2. KOO STARK AND PRINCE ANDREW

England's Prince Andrew met Koo Stark in February 1982. The daughter of film producer William Stark, Koo was attractive, intelligent, and had a proper sense of decorum. The royal family approved of her, and it appeared she might become a duchess, but the romance unraveled when the tabloids revealed Koo had appeared topless in *The Adventures of Emily.*

3. BELA LUGOSI AND CLARA BOW

Clara Bow met Bela Lugosi while he was starring on stage in *Dracula.* Bow told the press she was giving the Romanian elocution lessons; in reality, they were involved in a steamy love affair. Bela wanted to marry Clara, but she had other beaus. Lugosi kept a nude photo of Clara Bow in his home until his death in 1956.

4. ELIZABETH TAYLOR AND LARRY FORTENSKY

Of Elizabeth Taylor's seven husbands, the most unlikely was her last, Larry Fortensky. On October 6, 1991, Taylor and Fortensky were married at Michael Jackson's estate, Neverland. The 59-year-old bride was 20 years older than her new husband. The couple had met at an alcohol rehab center, and the construction worker seemed to be an unlikely mate for one of Hollywood's most glamorous stars.

5. GLORIA GRAHAME AND TONY RAY

Gloria Grahame, who won an Academy Award in 1952 for her supporting performance in *The Bad and the Beautiful,* was married to director Nicholas Ray when she became involved with Ray's teenage son, Tony. Grahame and Ray soon divorced, and, years later, the actress married Tony Ray.

6. MILTON BERLE AND AIMEE SEMPLE MCPHERSON

Comedian Milton Berle appeared in many films, including *It's a Mad, Mad, Mad, Mad World* and *The Loved One.* Berle revealed that, in his youth, he had a brief affair with Aimee

Semple McPherson. Sister Aimee was one of America's most popular evangelists until she staged her own disappearance to conceal another affair she was having.

7. MARLENE DIETRICH AND GENERAL GEORGE PATTON

Marlene Dietrich and George Patton were an unlikely couple. The German-born actress and the American general met each other during World War II. Patton gave Dietrich a pearl-handled pistol as a Christmas present in 1944. The pair was linked romantically, but Patton died after an automobile accident in 1945.

8. MARILYN MONROE AND ARTHUR MILLER

The marriage of Marilyn Monroe to Arthur Miller combined beauty and brains. Monroe was the number one sex symbol in the world, and Miller, who had authored acclaimed plays such as *Death of a Salesman* and *The Crucible,* was one of America's best writers. Monroe and Miller were married in 1956 and divorced in 1961.

9. GREER GARSON AND RICHARD NEY

Greer Garson won an Oscar in 1942 for her performance as the title character in the wartime drama *Mrs. Miniver.* Richard Ney played her son in the movie. Garson and Ney were married in 1943 and divorced a few years later.

10. MICHAEL JACKSON AND LISA MARIE PRESLEY

Few people believed it when Michael Jackson, the King of Pop, married Lisa Marie Presley, the daughter of the King of

Rock and Roll. The secret marriage took place on May 26, 1994, in the Dominican Republic. Few thought it would last, and they were right; Presley filed for divorce on February 1, 1996.

May-December Romances

Tony Curtis said the secret to youth was to marry someone much younger. Groucho Marx married Eden Hartford, a woman less than half his age. Martha Raye's last marriage was to a man more than 35 years younger than she. For these couples, age differences did not matter.

1. ANNA NICOLE SMITH AND HOWARD MARSHALL II

There were skeptics when 26-year-old actress Anna Nicole Smith married 89-year-old millionaire Howard Marshall II. Many accused Smith of marrying Marshall for his money. Smith denied the charges, saying she truly loved Marshall and had turned down numerous proposals from him before finally accepting. Marshall died a year later, in 1995, and the voluptuous Smith wore a low-cut dress to the memorial service. "I just tried to dress up for him," she said, "He loved my breasts." Although Smith reportedly inherited $480 million from Marshall's estate, the bequest was the subject of lengthy litigation between Marshall's sons and Smith.

2. TONY RANDALL AND HEATHER HARLAN

Tony Randall was 75 years old when he married 25-year-old Heather Harlan in November 1995. On April 11, 1997, Heather gave birth to a daughter, Julia, making the 77-year-old actor a father for the first time. A year later, Randall had his second child.

3. ANTHONY QUINN AND KATHY BENVIN

Two-time Oscar winner Anthony Quinn was 78 when he fathered a child with his 32-year-old secretary, Kathy Benvin. At the time, Quinn's oldest child was 52.

4. FRED ASTAIRE AND ROBYN SMITH

Fred Astaire was 74 years old when he met 31-year-old Robyn Smith, a successful jockey. The couple wed on June 7, 1980, and remained husband and wife until Astaire's death in 1987.

5. WOODY ALLEN AND SOON-YI PREVIN

In 1992, Mia Farrow discovered that her lover, Woody Allen, was having an affair with her adopted daughter, Soon-Yi Previn. Although there was a 35-year age difference between Allen and Previn, they were married in 1997, making Farrow Allen's mother-in-law.

6. CHARLIE CHAPLIN AND OONA O'NEILL

According to Charlie Chaplin, a young girl is "the most beautiful thing in the world," so it's not surprising most of Chaplin's romances were with teenage girls. His last wife,

Oona O'Neill, the daughter of noted playwright Eugene O'Neill, was 36 years younger than Chaplin.

7. CLINT EASTWOOD AND DINA RUIZ

Clint Eastwood, who has starred in films such as *Dirty Harry* and *The Unforgiven,* was 65 years old when he married 30-year-old news anchor Dina Ruiz on March 31, 1996. Eastwood's eldest daughter was two years older than his bride.

8. CARY GRANT AND DYAN CANNON

When Cary Grant married actress Dyan Cannon, on July 22, 1965, he was 61, 34 years older than his wife. The couple, who divorced on March 21, 1968, had one child—Jennifer.

9. HAYLEY MILLS AND RAY BOULTING

Hayley Mills was the most popular actress of the early 1960s. The daughter of British actor John Mills was 18 years old in 1966 when she starred in her first adult role in the film *The Family Way.* During filming, Mills fell in love with her 52-year-old director, Ray Boulting. When Hayley marred the older man, in 1971, she received hate mail from heartbroken young men all over the world. The actress and the director divorced in 1976.

10. HUMPHREY BOGART AND LAUREN BACALL

Humphrey Bogart fell in love with 20-year-old costar Lauren Bacall during filming of *To Have and Have Not.* They were known as Bogey and Baby, and, despite their 25-year age difference, Bogart and Bacall were happily married until his death in 1957.

It Can't Be Love

Johnny Carson joked, "Why do Hollywood divorces cost so much? Because they're worth it." Many Hollywood couples do not end up living happily ever after. In 1969, Rory Calhoun's wife, Lita Baron, sued the actor for divorce, citing his adultery with 79 different women. Sharon Stone compared ex-boyfriend Dwight Yoakam to a "dirt sandwich." The marriage of Sean Penn and Madonna was one of the stormiest in Hollywood history.

1. CHARLIE CHAPLIN AND LITA GREY

In 1924, Charlie Chaplin married 16-year-old Lita Grey; the young actress had become pregnant while filming *The Gold Rush*. On their wedding night, however, Chaplin reportedly asked his wife to throw herself beneath the wheels of the train on which they were returning from their honeymoon in Mexico. The 1927 divorce was even more disastrous to Chaplin. Grey accused Chaplin of at least five cases of adultery and revealed intimate details of her sex life with Chaplin. Thousands of transcripts of the sensational trial were sold. The stress of the divorce caused Chaplin's hair to turn gray overnight.

2. ZSA ZSA GABOR AND GEORGE SANDERS

George Sanders's five-year marriage to Zsa Zsa Gabor was stormy. Sanders said he felt like a guest in their Bel Air mansion, that most of the house was filled with photographs of and clippings about Zsa Zsa. The final straw came on Christmas Eve, when Sanders caught his wife with the notorious playboy Porfirio Rubirosa. In the holiday spirit, Sanders threw a gift-wrapped brick through the bedroom window, then threw open the door and exclaimed, "Merry Christmas, my dear."

3. JOAN COLLINS AND MAXWELL REED

Joan Collins was 18 years old when she married British actor Maxwell Reed. According to Collins, Reed slipped her a mickey and raped her on their first date. After they were married, Reed offered to sell a night of sex with his wife to a wealthy Arab sheik for $10,000. Collins rejected the indecent proposal and filed for divorce soon thereafter.

4. JOAN COLLINS AND PETER HOLM

More than 30 years after her disastrous marriage to Maxwell Reed, Joan Collins went through a painful divorce from Peter Holm. Collins filed for divorce when she learned Holm had been having an affair with an Italian beauty, Romina Danielson, known as The Passion Flower. On July 16, 1987, Holm picketed Collins's mansion, claiming he was homeless. The bitter divorce ended with Holm accepting a settlement of only a fraction of what he was demanding.

5. LUPE VELEZ AND BIG BOY WILLIAMS

Guinn "Big Boy" Williams was a popular character actor, whose nickname was appropriate for the powerful 250 pounder. In 1940, Williams became engaged to Lupe Velez, the fiery Mexican spitfire. Velez and Williams became involved in a quarrel at Errol Flynn's house; Velez picked up a photograph of Williams and broke the frame over Big Boy's head. She then yanked the photo out of the frame, tore it into little pieces, and threw it on the floor. Finally, she urinated on it.

6. ED WOOD AND NORMA MCCARTY

Ed Wood earned his dubious reputation as the world's worst director with films such as *Plan 9 from Outer Space* and *Glen or Glenda?* He married Norma McCarty in a ceremony on the Sunset sound stage. The marriage was short-lived, however, after Mrs. Wood discovered her husband dressed in a nightgown and high heels. She was unaware that Wood liked to dress in women's clothing.

7. CLARA BOW AND ROBERT SAVAGE

Clara Bow had a brief romance with Yale football player Robert Savage. When they broke up, Savage slashed his wrists and dripped blood on the photo of his former lover. When Bow was informed of the suicide attempt, she exclaimed, "Real men don't slash their wrists, they use guns." Savage survived the suicide attempt.

8. ROSEANNE AND TOM ARNOLD

The divorce of Roseanne and Tom Arnold was one of the most vituperative in Hollywood history. Roseanne summed up her feelings when she said, "I'm not upset about my divorce, I'm only upset that I'm not a widow." She has since filed for divorce from Arnold's successor.

9. **HUMPHREY BOGART AND MAYO METHOT**

Humphrey Bogart married Mayo Methot in 1938. They became known as the Battling Bogarts, and their altercations often took place in public. Frequently, the quarrels led to blows. Mayo, whom Bogart nicknamed "Sluggy," would warn Bogart of an imminent attack by singing "Embraceable You."

10. **DENNIS HOPPER AND MICHELLE PHILLIPS**

On October 31, 1970, Dennis Hopper married singer-actress Michelle Phillips, former wife of the Mamas and the Papas' John Phillips. Shortly after the wedding, Phillips went on a singing tour. Hopper received a call from Phillips eight days later informing him that she was leaving him. Reportedly, Phillips asked Hopper if he had ever considered suicide.

The Marrying Kind

S ilent film actress Barbara La Marr was married six times before her death at 29. Hedy Lamarr also walked down the aisle six times. Johnny Weissmuller, who played Tarzan in the movies, had six Janes in real life. When at first you don't succeed, marry, marry again.

1. ZSA ZSA GABOR

Oscar Levant quipped, "Marriage is for bores—I mean Gabors." At last count, Zsa Zsa Gabor has been married eight times. When asked how many husbands she has had, Zsa Zsa replied, "You mean apart from my own? I believe in large families. . . . Every woman should have at least three husbands." Her former husbands include actor George Sanders and hotel tycoon Conrad Hilton. In 1977, Zsa Zsa married her divorce lawyer, Michael O'Hara; they divorced five years later. Gabor lamented, "It's never easy keeping your husband happy. It's much easier to make someone else's husband happy." According to Zsa Zsa, getting married is just the first step toward getting a divorce.

2. ELIZABETH TAYLOR

Wit Oscar Levant joked about Elizabeth Taylor: "Always a bride, never a bridesmaid." Taylor has been married eight times to seven men. After each wedding, she declared she was unbelievably happy and the marriage would last forever. The list of her former husbands includes actors Michael Wilding and Richard Burton, singer Eddie Fisher, producer Mike Todd, and Senator John Warner. Taylor and Burton were married twice. During the ceremony for her sixth marriage, the justice of the peace asked Taylor the names of her former husbands. "What is this, a memory test?" she snapped.

3. MICKEY ROONEY

Mickey Rooney said, "I'm the only man whose marriage license reads: 'To whom it may concern.'" Rooney was married eight times. Two of his ex-wives were actresses Ava Gardner and Martha Vickers. Rooney expressed no regrets, claiming he'd marry them all again.

4. LANA TURNER

Lana Turner was another movie star who married eight times. Actor Lex Barker and musician Artie Shaw were two of Turner's former husbands. Shaw was also married seven times.

5. STAN LAUREL

Stan Laurel of the comedy team Laurel and Hardy married eight times, including twice to Virginia Rogers. His final marriage, to actress Ida Raphael, lasted 18 years, until his death.

6. **MARIE McDONALD**

Marie "The Body" McDonald died of a drug overdose at age 42 in 1965. In her short life, she was married seven times. She once said, "Husbands are easier to find than good agents."

7. **TONY CURTIS**

Tony Curtis's five wives included actresses Janet Leigh and Christine Kaufmann. Curtis explained his marriage failures: "Marriage is very difficult. Very few of us are fortunate enough to marry multimillionaires with 39-inch busts and [who] have undergone frontal lobotomies."

8. **BETTE DAVIS**

Bette Davis married four times. Her last marriage, to actor Gary Merrill, ended in divorce in 1960. In Davis's words, none of her husbands was man enough to be Mrs. Bette Davis. In later years, Davis said she would consider marrying again if she "found a man who had $15 million and would sign over half to me before the marriage and guarantee he'd be dead within a year."

9. **JUDY GARLAND**

Judy Garland married four times. Her second marriage, to director Vincente Minnelli, produced Liza, born in 1946. Garland invited Liza to her fifth wedding, to Mickey Dean, in March 1969. Liza sent her a message: "Can't make it, but I'll promise to come to your next one." There would be no next one; Garland was found dead in her London apartment three months later.

10. CLAUDE RAINS

Claude Rains was an outstanding character actor who is best remembered for his role as Louis Renault, the corrupt official in *Casablanca*. Rains was married seven times. His longest-lasting marriage, to actress Frances Propper, lasted 21 years. He was also married to two other actresses: Isabel Jeans and Marie Hemingway.

Role Reversals

Stars are offered many roles. Occasionally, they turn down some they later wish they hadn't. W. C. Fields turned down the title role in *The Wizard of Oz* because he wanted more money. Robert Montgomery turned down the male lead in *It Happened One Night,* a role for which Clark Gable won an Academy Award. Burt Lancaster turned down the role of Ben-Hur because he thought he looked ridiculous in the Roman costume. Charlton Heston won an Oscar for his portrayal of Ben-Hur. Bela Lugosi turned down the part of Frankenstein's monster, a role that made his horror rival, Boris Karloff, a star. Sometimes, the first choices for a role are hard to believe. Mae West was asked to play fading star Norma Desmond in *Sunset Boulevard.* Doris Day was considered for the role of Mrs. Robinson in *The Graduate.* The original duo for the "Road" pictures made famous by Bob Hope and Bing Crosby was Fred MacMurray and Jack Oakie. James Cagney was scheduled to play Robin Hood until he walked out in a contract dispute and was replaced by Errol Flynn. Believe it or not, the first choice to play Archie Bunker in the television series *All in the Family* was Mickey Rooney.

1. **GEORGE RAFT**

No one exercised worse judgment in choosing films than George Raft. Within a two-year period, he turned down *High Sierra, The Maltese Falcon,* and *Casablanca.* Humphrey Bogart played all three roles, and they made him a star. Raft turned down *High Sierra* because his character, Roy Earl, died at the end of the picture. He refused to do *The Maltese Falcon* because he did not consider it to be an important film. His reasoning for turning down *Casablanca* was that he didn't want to star opposite some "unknown Swedish broad." That unknown Swedish broad was Ingrid Bergman, who teamed with Bogart to turn *Casablanca* into a film classic.

2. **HEDY LAMARR**

Hedy Lamarr unwisely turned down the role of Ilsa in *Casablanca* because the script was not finished. Ingrid Bergman took the part and it made her a star. The next year, Lamarr turned down the lead in *Gaslight.* Once again, Bergman accepted the part and won her first Academy Award.

3. **JAMES CAAN**

In the 1970s, James Caan turned down roles in a series of blockbuster films. Caan was offered the leading roles in *One Flew Over the Cuckoo's Nest* and *Kramer vs. Kramer,* films that earned Oscars for Jack Nicholson and Dustin Hoffman. Caan also turned down the role of Superman, which made a star of Christopher Reeve.

4. **NORMA SHEARER**

Norma Shearer turned down the role of Scarlett O'Hara because she didn't feel the role was right for her. Vivien

Leigh played the part and won an Oscar. Three years later, Shearer turned down the title role in *Mrs. Miniver* because she didn't want to play a mother. Greer Garson accepted the part and won an Oscar.

5. **TUESDAY WELD**

Tuesday Weld has turned down a number of choice roles, including that of Bonnie Parker in *Bonnie and Clyde.* Faye Dunaway received her first Oscar nomination for her performance as the bank robber. Weld also was the first choice to play the mother of Satan's child in *Rosemary's Baby,* which went to Mia Farrow.

6. **RONALD REAGAN**

Ronald Reagan was considered seriously for the role of Rick in *Casablanca,* and Ann Sheridan, Reagan's costar in *Kings Row,* was considered to star opposite Reagan. Instead, the roles were played by Humphrey Bogart and Ingrid Bergman, whose screen chemistry helped to make *Casablanca* a classic.

7. **ROBERT REDFORD**

Robert Redford had his choice of roles in the 1960s and 1970s, and he occasionally let a good role get away. Three films that Redford turned down were *Who's Afraid of Virginia Woolf, The Graduate,* and *Love Story.* The roles went to George Segal, Dustin Hoffman, and Ryan O'Neal.

8. **BRIGITTE HELM**

Brigitte Helm, a German actress who starred in *Metropolis,* turned down the role of Lola Lola in *The Blue Angel,* a film directed by Josef von Sternberg. The role went to Marlene Dietrich, who starred in a series of films directed by Sternberg. Helm never became a star in the United States.

9. **TOM SELLECK**

Tom Selleck was Steven Spielberg's first choice to play Indiana Jones in *Raiders of the Lost Ark,* but the shooting schedule for the film conflicted with Selleck's television series, *Magnum P.I.* Harrison Ford was brought in to play the role, and the film became one of the biggest box office blockbusters in the history of the cinema.

10. **GEORGE JESSEL**

George Jessel, who was offered the lead role in *The Jazz Singer,* the first talking picture, asked for $40,000, but was offered $30,000. Jessel refused, and Al Jolson eventually was paid $75,000 to star in the film.

Miscast

Even the best actor can look bad if he or she is miscast. Paul Newman has always been embarrassed by his film debut in *The Silver Chalice*. Michael Jackson has expressed his desire to portray author Edgar Allan Poe on screen. If he does, he will be the latest actor to be miscast in a film.

1. JOHN WAYNE

John Wayne asked to play the role of the Mongol warrior Genghis Khan, in the 1955 film *The Conqueror*. The Duke told the press he considered the movie to be a western and Genghis Khan was like a gunfighter. Wayne made no attempt to play the role any different from how he played cowboys in his westerns. As a result, the performance was laughable, and the film was a disaster.

2. HARPO MARX

Unbelievably, Harpo Marx was cast to play the brilliant English scientist, Sir Isaac Newton, in the 1957 film, *The Story of Mankind*. Instead of having an apple drop on Newton's head, a whole bushel of apples fell on Harpo's head for comic effect. Marx was not the only bit of unusual casting in the film; Dennis Hopper portrayed Napoleon.

3. **MICKEY ROONEY**

In *The Private Lives of Adam and Eve,* Mickey Rooney played the role of the Devil, which might have been the low point of Rooney's long career. Another highlight of the film was sexpot Mamie Van Doren's portrayal of Eve. Van Doren, already known for her ample bustline, wore an outfit with lifelike rubber balloons over her breasts. The film was condemned by The Catholic Legion of Decency and panned universally by critics.

4. **HUMPHREY BOGART**

Humphrey Bogart as a zombie? Bogart played an executed man who returned to life in the 1938 film *The Return of Dr. X.* Happily, it was Bogart's only appearance in a horror film.

5. **LUCIANO PAVAROTTI**

Luciano Pavarotti may be one of the best tenors in the world, but he's certainly not the best actor. In 1982, Pavarotti starred in the film *Yes, Giorgio,* playing—what else?—an Italian tenor. After seeing the film, audiences exclaimed, "No, Giorgio."

6. **RAY MILLAND**

Ray Milland had a long and distinguished acting career. In 1945, he won the Academy Award for Best Actor for his portrayal of an alcoholic in *The Lost Weekend.* He gave his most embarrassing performance in the 1972 film *The Thing with Two Heads,* however. Milland played a doctor who has his head transplanted onto Rosey Grier's body. It's not surprising that Milland has a look of disgust on his face throughout the movie, probably because he was wondering why he had ever agreed to appear in this turkey.

7. **CARY GRANT**

Charming Cary Grant rarely gave a bad performance, but one of his worst was as Cole Porter in the 1945 film *Night and Day*. Grant sang off-key and was totally miscast as the Indiana-born composer. Grant was so upset with director Michael Curtiz, he told him, "If I'm ever stupid enough to be caught working with you again, you'll know I'm either broke or I've lost my mind."

8. **ROGER DALTREY**

Director Ken Russell developed a reputation for his unconventional casting. One of his oddest choices was Roger Daltrey, lead singer of the rock group The Who, to portray the nineteenth-century pianist-composer, Franz Liszt, in the 1975 film *Lisztomania*.

9. **TONY CURTIS**

One of the classic examples of miscasting was Tony Curtis's role of Antoninus in Stanley Kubrick's Roman epic, *Spartacus*. Curtis's heavy Bronx accent clearly was inappropriate for the role.

10. **VAL KILMER**

Val Kilmer starred in *Batman Forever* and *The Doors*. Kilmer was cast against type when he portrayed modern artist Willem de Kooning in Ed Harris's 2000 film, *Pollock*. A film reviewer in *The New Yorker* accurately described Kilmer as "pretending to be Willem de Kooning."

Method to Their Madness

John Barrymore once said, "There are lots of methods of acting. Mine involves a lot of talent, a glass, and some cracked ice." Method actors will go to any extreme to become the characters they play. Lynn Redgrave gained 50 pounds for her Oscar-nominated performance in *Georgy Girl*. Gary Oldman starved himself so much to play punk rocker Sid Vicious in *Sid and Nancy* that he was treated in a hospital for malnutrition. John Goodman joked, "It's pretty sad when a person has to lose weight to play Babe Ruth."

1. NICOLAS CAGE

Nicolas Cage won an Academy Award for his portrayal of a self-destructive alcoholic in *Leaving Las Vegas*. Cage will subject himself to anything to make his performance more convincing. He reportedly spent time getting drunk preparing for his role in *Leaving Las Vegas*, and, to feel the pain of a wounded soldier in *Racing with the Moon*, he slashed his arm with a knife. Cage had two teeth pulled without novocaine to resemble the character he played in *Birdy*. Perhaps his most outrageous act was eating six live cockroaches in *Vampire's Kiss*.

2. ROBERT DE NIRO

The ultimate method actor, Robert De Niro turned down the role of Christ in *The Last Temptation of Christ* because he couldn't envision the role. He won an Oscar in 1980 for his portrayal of boxing champion Jake La Motta in *Raging Bull*, for which he gained 60 pounds to play the out-of-shape former champ in his later years. For his role as Al Capone in *The Untouchables*, De Niro had a tailor make him silk underwear similar to the kind Capone wore.

3. JAMES DEAN

During the early shooting of *Giant*, James Dean admitted to being nervous in his scenes with Elizabeth Taylor. Unexpectedly, in front of 4,000 spectators who had gathered to watch the filming, Dean pulled down his zipper and urinated. When his friend, Dennis Hopper, asked him why he did it, Dean replied that if he could urinate in front of a crowd, playing a scene with Elizabeth Taylor would be easy.

4. HALLE BERRY

Halle Berry had to conceal her glamorous image to play a crackhead in Spike Lee's *Jungle Fever*. She achieved the feeling of being a drug addict by not bathing for days.

5. MARLON BRANDO

Marlon Brando was the actor who popularized the method approach to acting. To prepare himself to play the role of a

The usually glamorous Halle Berry proved her range as an actress by playing a crack addict in Spike Lee's *Jungle Fever* (1991).

Photofest

paraplegic in the 1950 film *The Men,* Brando spent a month in a wheelchair in the Van Nuys Hospital for Paraplegics.

6. **MARTIN SHEEN**

Martin Sheen remained drunk for two days to play the opening scene in the 1979 film *Apocalypse Now.* The strenuous shoot proved nearly fatal: during the filming, Sheen suffered a heart attack.

7. **LILLIAN GISH**

Lillian Gish wanted her death scene in the 1926 film *La Bohéme* to be believable, so she went to a hospital to study patients with lung disease. Gish learned how to stop breathing in such a convincing manner that director King Vidor was momentarily concerned that she had died.

8. **DANIEL DAY LEWIS**

Academy Award winner Daniel Day Lewis slept in a phony jail cell in Dublin to prepare for his role as an imprisoned man in the film *In the Name of the Father.* He lost 30 pounds on a diet of prison food and even instructed the crew to abuse him so he could better understand how a prisoner might feel.

9. **RUSSELL CROWE**

Russell Crowe won an Academy Award for Best Actor in 2001 for his performance in *Gladiator.* When Crowe was filming the 1992 Australian drama *Romper Stomper* he was pulled over repeatedly by police, who thought he was a real skinhead.

Academy Award–winning actor Russell Crowe has proven controversial both on and off the big screen.

10. DUSTIN HOFFMAN

For *Marathon Man,* a 1976 film starring Dustin Hoffman and Laurence Olivier, Hoffman stayed awake for a few days to play a scene in which he was supposed to be exhausted. Olivier, astonished by Hoffman's unorthodox technique, asked, "Dear boy, why don't you just learn to act?"

Star Behavior

Some actors insist on receiving the star treatment. On a trip to Europe, Ginger Rogers brought along 118 pieces of luggage. Barbra Streisand insisted on peach-colored toilet paper while staying at a hotel. Bing Crosby had an ermine-covered toilet seat.

1. JOAN CRAWFORD

Nobody personified movie star behavior better than Joan Crawford, who said, "I never go out unless I look like Joan Crawford, the movie star." Shelley Winters said of Crawford, "My idea of a movie star is Joan Crawford, who can chew up two directors and three producers before lunch." Crawford wore a special dress when she sat down to answer her fan mail three times a week. When asked why she didn't hire a secretary to sign her name, she replied, "Because there is only one Joan Crawford." When she dated attorney Greg Bautzer, she insisted he walk two steps behind her in public. One time Crawford arrived at a party at Jerry Wald's house with a diamond in the middle of her forehead. Crawford had placed the gem there so no one would notice the bags under her eyes.

2. ZSA ZSA GABOR

Gossip columnist Louella Parsons said of Zsa Zsa Gabor, "She can make more fuss about nothing than anyone in Hollywood." Nobody could make an entrance like Zsa Zsa. When she ate at the exclusive Pump Room restaurant in Chicago's Ambassador Hotel, she would call first to make certain there was a full crowd to view her entrance.

3. ERROL FLYNN

Errol Flynn enjoyed being the center of attention, on and off the screen. On a trip to Cuba in the 1930s, Flynn hired a full orchestra to accompany him wherever he went.

4. RUDY VALLEE

Rudy Vallee, who starred in the 1942 Preston Sturges comedy, *The Palm Beach Story*, tried to get the name of the street he lived on changed to Rue de Vallee. He was indignant when the other residents of the street refused to allow the name to be changed.

5. BETTE DAVIS

Bette Davis made it clear that she was the star of any movie in which she appeared; there wasn't a picture big enough for Davis and a top leading man. She avoided co-starring with stars of equal stature, such as Clark Gable, Cary Grant, or Gary Cooper. Even when her star began to fade, Davis still demanded respect. When a young actress asked her what Hollywood was like in her era, Davis replied, "My era will end when they put me in the grave."

6. **FRANK SINATRA**

Frank Sinatra had his moments of boorish behavior. Actress Valerie Perrine recalled seeing Sinatra gambling in a Las Vegas casino. Sinatra kicked a couple of bottles of champagne in the direction of an elderly woman who was playing a slot machine near The Chairman of the Board, saying, "Get away! You're bothering me."

7. **PAUL MUNI**

Paul Muni was one of the biggest stars of the 1930s, and he made certain everybody knew it. He posted his wife outside of his dressing room, so if anyone tried to see him, the person was told, "Mr. Muni does not communicate with anyone."

8. **MARION DAVIES**

Dressing rooms are status symbols for movie stars. Normally, the bigger the star, the bigger the dressing room. The exception was Marion Davies, who, although never a major star, had the largest dressing room in Hollywood, thanks to her lover, William Randolph Hearst. In 1926, a 14-room Mediterranean-style bungalow was built for Davies at the MGM studio. The rooms were furnished with antiques, and Davies's whims were catered to by a staff of servants. When Davies left MGM for Warner Brothers, her dressing room was taken apart piece by piece and reassembled at Warner.

9. **DEMI MOORE**

Really big stars get their way no matter the cost. In 1995, Demi Moore had a scene in *The Scarlet Letter* reshot at the cost of $100,000 because she didn't like the way her hair looked. Although her hair did look great after the reshoot, the film was a box office disappointment.

10. GLORIA SWANSON

At the peak of her popularity in the 1920s, no star lived more extravagantly than Gloria Swanson. She spent up to $125,000 a year on clothes, $10,000 a year on lingerie, and another $9,000 on stockings.

Oscar Oddities

The annual Academy Awards ceremonies have been known for their inane musical production numbers and endless length. They also have had more than their share of odd moments. At the 1937 Oscar ceremony, when Charlie McCarthy was given an honorary wooden Oscar, the wooden dummy of ventriloquist Edgar Bergen asked for a gold Oscar if one was left over. That same year, the Oscar Spencer Tracy was given for his performance in *Captains Courageous* was inscribed to Dick Tracy.

1. DAVID NIVEN

David Niven was attempting to present an award at the 1974 Oscar ceremony when a streaker named Robert Opel ran behind him. The unflappable Englishman observed, "Just think—the only laugh that man will probably get is for stripping and showing his shortcomings."

2. CHILL WILLS

Chill Wills was nominated for an Academy Award for his supporting performance in *The Alamo*. Wills launched the most outrageous campaign in Oscar history in a vain attempt to win the award. As part of his effort, he bought a large ad in the trade papers that read, "All my Alamo buddies are praying for me to win more than the real Alamo fighters prayed for their lives." A disgusted Groucho Marx took out an ad that said, "Dear Chill, I'm voting for Sal Mineo." Mineo was also nominated for his performance in *Exodus*. Wills's campaign probably cost him votes, and Peter Ustinov won the award for his role in *Spartacus*.

3. **FRANK CAPRA**

Probably the most embarrassing moment in Oscar history came at the 1933 awards ceremony. Will Rogers was the presenter for the Best Director Oscar. Rogers opened the envelope and said, "It couldn't happen to a nicer guy; come up and get it, Frank." Frank Capra, who was nominated for directing *Lady for a Day*, was halfway up to the stage before he realized the winner was Frank Lloyd for *Cavalcade*. The next year, Capra won the Oscar for his direction of *It Happened One Night*.

4. **TUESDAY WELD**

At the 1964 Academy Awards ceremony, presenter Tuesday Weld wore a bouffant hairstyle, similar to the one popularized by former First Lady Jacqueline Kennedy. As Weld read the nominees for Best Sound Effects, her hairstyle collapsed in her face.

5. **MARLON BRANDO**

Marlon Brando won his first Academy Award in 1954 for his performance in *On the Waterfront*. In 1969, he asked the Academy for a replacement when the statue was stolen. In

Actress Tuesday Weld.

1972, Brando won his second Oscar for his portrayal of a Mafia don in *The Godfather.* The unpredictable Brando declined the Oscar. When his name was announced, a Native American named Sacheen Littlefeather (actually actress Maria Cruz) gave a speech protesting the movie industry's depiction of Native Americans.

6. **ROBERT RICH**

The 1956 Oscar for original screenplay was awarded to Robert Rich for his work on *The Brave One.* Nineteen years later, it was learned that Robert Rich was actually the blacklisted writer, Dalton Trumbo.

7. **ELWOOD ULLMAN AND EDWARD BERNDS**

The Academy announced that Elwood Ullman and Edward Bernds were nominated for an Oscar in 1957 for their story for the film *High Society.* It came as quite a shock, since the film was a Bowery Boys comedy. The real nominee was John Patrick, for another film named *High Society.*

8. **P. H. VAZAK**

Screenwriter Robert Towne was unhappy when director Hugh Hudson brought in another writer, Michael Austin, to work on the screenplay for *Greystoke: The Legend of Tarzan.* When the screenplay was nominated for an Oscar, Towne listed P. H. Vazak as a cowriter. What the Academy didn't know was that P. H. Vazak was Towne's dog. The Academy was saved further embarrassment when *Greystoke* did not win the best screenplay Oscar.

9. **STAN BERMAN**

Stan Berman billed himself as the world's greatest gate-crasher. Berman grabbed the microphone at the 1961 Academy Awards ceremony from presenter Shelley Winters and told the shocked audience he was there to present host Bob Hope with a handmade statue. Hope had joked for years about never receiving an Oscar for his acting.

10. **JERRY LEWIS**

Believe it or not, the 1958 Oscar telecast actually finished 20 minutes ahead of schedule, so host Jerry Lewis was told to improvise to fill the time. Lewis did his best, mugging and directing the orchestra, until NBC mercifully cut away to a sports review program.

Actors Who Never Won an Oscar

M any of Hollywood's biggest stars never won an Academy Award in an acting category. Marlene Dietrich, Gloria Swanson, Barbara Stanwyck, Rita Hayworth, Montgomery Clift, James Dean, and Edward G. Robinson are some of the stars who never received the golden statue.

1. CARY GRANT

Cary Grant was the ultimate leading man, but his talents were never recognized with an Oscar. He was nominated for Best Actor in 1941 for *Penny Serenade* and in 1944 for *None But the Lonely Heart.* However, he wasn't even nominated for superior performances in *Holiday, Bringing Up Baby, His Girl Friday,* and *North by Northwest.*

2. MARILYN MONROE

Screen goddess Marilyn Monroe was never nominated for an Academy Award. Her two most overlooked performances were in the 1956 film *Bus Stop* and the 1959 classic *Some Like It Hot.*

3. **GRETA GARBO**

Another screen legend who never won an Oscar was Greta Garbo. Garbo was nominated for *Anna Christie, Romance, Camille,* and *Ninotchka,* but never received the award.

4. **KIRK DOUGLAS**

Kirk Douglas gave many powerful performances, but was never rewarded with the Oscar. Douglas received Best Actor nominations for *Champion, The Bad and the Beautiful,* and *Lust for Life.* When he turned down the role of a drunken gun-fighter in the 1965 film *Cat Ballou,* Lee Marvin took the part and won the Oscar.

5. **PETER O'TOOLE**

It's incredible that Peter O'Toole has never won an Academy Award. O'Toole was nominated seven times, including for his bravura performance in the 1962 film *Lawrence of Arabia,* but he never took home the Oscar.

6. **RICHARD BURTON**

Richard Burton shares the record for Oscar futility with Peter O'Toole. Between 1952 and 1979, Burton received seven Oscar nominations without a win. In 1966, Burton was nominated and lost for *Who's Afraid of Virginia Woolf?* His wife, Elizabeth Taylor, took home the Oscar for Best Actress in that same film.

7. **DEBORAH KERR**

The dubious record for the most nominations for best actress without a win belongs to Deborah Kerr. Kerr was nominated six times between 1949 and 1960, and two of the films for which she was nominated were *From Here to Eternity* and *The King and I.*

8. JUDY GARLAND

Judy Garland received two Oscar nominations for her performances in *A Star Is Born* and *Judgment at Nuremburg.* She lost both times. Garland was not nominated for either *The Wizard of Oz* or *Meet Me in St. Louis.*

9. NATALIE WOOD

Natalie Wood gave a series of memorable performances during the 1960s, but was never rewarded with an Oscar. Wood received nominations for *Rebel Without a Cause, Splendor in the Grass,* and *Love with the Proper Stranger.*

10. ROSALIND RUSSELL

Rosalind Russell was nominated four times for an Academy Award, but never won. In 1947, it was a forgone conclusion that she would win the Oscar for her performance in *Mourning Becomes Electra.* The early edition of the *Los Angeles Times* ran the headline; "ROZ RUSSELL WINS OSCAR." Nearly everyone was shocked when it was announced that Loretta Young had won for *The Farmer's Daughter.*

Photofest

Legendary actress Natalie Wood achieved great fame during her career although she never captured an Oscar. She died in a mysterious drowning accident in 1981 while on a yacht with husband Robert Wagner.

Hollywood's Most Embarrassing Moments

Marlene Dietrich had to do 236 takes of a scene in *Blue Angel* because the German actress was unable to pronounce the word "moths" correctly. Three-time Oscar winner Jack Nicholson froze during his first screen test and forgot all his lines. Here are some more of Hollywood's most embarrassing moments.

1. BILL COSBY

Bill Cosby produced and starred in the spy spoof *Leonard, Part 6.* Cosby was so unhappy with it he offered to buy the $20 million picture from Columbia Studios to keep it from being released. Unsuccessful, he asked the public not to see the film. "I'm not too big to admit when I've made a bomb," Cosby said.

2. JACKIE GLEASON

On January 20, 1961, Jackie Gleason hosted a game show, named *You're in the Picture.* The premise was that contestants would stick their heads through cutouts while the panelists tried to guess what the scene represented. The show was so bad that, the next week, Gleason spent an entire program apologizing for the fiasco. The show was canceled and replaced with *The Jackie Gleason Show*, on which Gleason interviewed celebrities.

3. **PETER BOGDANOVICH**

Peter Bogdanovich directed critically acclaimed films such as *The Last Picture Show* and *Targets.* He was less successful when he attempted a musical, *At Long Last Love.* The 1975 film, starring Burt Reynolds and Cybill Shepherd, was universally panned. Not even Cole Porter songs could save the film. Bogdanovich took out a full page ad in *The Hollywood Reporter* apologizing for the turkey.

4. **GREER GARSON**

Academy Award winner Greer Garson once took 125 takes to say the word "no" in the 1947 film *Desire.* Costar Robert Mitchum said, "I gave up being serious about motion pictures when I made a film with Greer Garson, and she took 125 takes to say 'no.'"

5. **JOAN CRAWFORD**

Before she became a star, Joan Crawford made a few nudie stag films, such as *The Casting Couch.* Reportedly, she and MGM spent a half-million dollars trying to buy up and destroy all the prints. Unfortunately for Crawford, she was never able to destroy them all.

6. **CLARK GABLE**

Clark Gable wore dentures and sometimes had extremely bad breath. Vivien Leigh refused to do love scenes with him in *Gone With the Wind* until he did something about his breath.

7. **RICHARD CHAMBERLAIN**

At the 1990 Deauville Film Festival, Richard Chamberlain was asked which French director he would most like to work with. Chamberlain replied, "François Truffaut," referring to the acclaimed director of *Jules and Jim, The 400 Blows,* and *Shoot the Piano Player.* The only problem was, Truffaut had been dead for six years.

8. **ALAN LADD**

Alan Ladd was one of the shortest leading men in Hollywood, and studios were forced to come up with ingenious ways to make him appear taller than his costars. In the film *Boy on a Dolphin,* Ladd was forced to stand on a box in scenes with Sophia Loren. On another occasion, an actress playing opposite Ladd was forced to stand in a trench.

9. **EDWARD G. ROBINSON**

Edward G. Robinson was superb at playing gangsters, but winced every time he heard gunshots. During the filming of *Little Caesar,* director Mervyn LeRoy taped Robinson's eyelids open.

10. **JOHNNY DEPP**

Johnny Depp tattooed "Winona Forever" on his body when he was dating actress Winona Ryder. After they broke up, Depp came up with a unique solution. He changed the tattoo to read: "Wino Forever."

Nobody's Perfect

In Hollywood, it's essential for stars to look their best. Sometimes actors undergo cosmetic surgery to improve their looks. Face-lifts, breast enhancements, breast reductions, collagen lip injections, capped teeth, toupees, hair implants, nose jobs, liposuction, tummy tucks, and butt-lifts are just a few of the things that make stars look their best.

1. SYLVESTER STALLONE

During delivery, Sylvester Stallone had a nerve in his face severed by the doctor's forceps. The nerve damage partially paralyzed his lips and chin, so, to correct the condition, Stallone had a half-face-lift.

2. SEAN CONNERY

In his later films, Sean Connery wore a toupee to cover his baldness. For the 1983 James Bond film, *Never Say Never Again*, Connery wore a specially fitted toupee that cost $57,000.

3. RITA CAREWE

Rita Carewe, a blonde actress of the 1920s, she had her legs polished to give the appearance of wearing silk stockings.

4. MARILYN MONROE

Marilyn Monroe was one of many actresses to have cosmetic surgery to improve her appearance. Early in her career, Monroe had plastic surgery on her nose and chin, and had cartilage added to her jaw. She also had her teeth fixed and hairline raised.

5. MARLENE DIETRICH

Marlene Dietrich rivaled Greta Garbo as the Golden Age of Hollywood's most glamorous star. Dietrich was admired particularly for her high cheekbones, but few knew Dietrich achieved her sunken cheek look by having two of her upper rear molars removed.

6. RAQUEL WELCH

According to makeup artist George Masters, Raquel Welch is "silicone from the knees up." Groucho Marx joked, "I believe Miss Raquel Welch got her good looks from her father. He is a plastic surgeon, isn't he?"

7. DEAN MARTIN

Dean Martin had successful careers in the movies, music, and television. He teamed with Jerry Lewis in a series of film comedies, and he soloed in such films as *Rio Bravo* and *Some Came Running.* Before Martin had rhinoplasty, he had an exceptionally long nose. Comedian Alan King said that before Martin had the surgery, he looked like he was eating a banana.

8. **CLAUDETTE COLBERT**

Claudette Colbert won an Academy Award in 1934 for her performance in *It Happened One Night.* Because Colbert had a flaw on the right side of her face, she demanded that she usually be shot from her good side. The right side of her face was seen so rarely on film it was referred to on the set as the "dark side of the moon."

9. **NATALIE WOOD**

Natalie Wood was a beautiful actress, but she did have one imperfection she tried to conceal from the public—a deformed left wrist. She had a clause in her contract that the studio had to provide bracelets to cover the blemish when she appeared in films.

10. **BING CROSBY**

Bing Crosby was a popular crooner when he came to Hollywood in 1930. Studio executives were concerned, however, that his ears were too big for him to become a star, so spirit gum was used to glue his ears back.

Strange Behavior

People in the movie industry have never been known for their conventional behavior. These performers had their own idiosyncrasies.

1. CECIL B. DE MILLE

During his career, Cecil B. De Mille directed many of Hollywood's most expensive epics. In real life, De Mille had a phobia about touching used currency; he sent his secretary to the bank several times a day to get new bills.

2. JOAN CRAWFORD

After she became a star, Joan Crawford developed a phobia about cleanliness. When she gave parties in her home, Crawford followed her guests and carefully wiped the doorknobs they had touched. Once she warned producer Ross Hunter about sitting in a chair: "Not there," she said, "Loretta Young just sat there."

3. MACK SENNETT

Mack Sennett was a comic genius who created the Keystone Cops and helped launch the film careers of Charlie Chaplin,

Mabel Normand, Fatty Arbuckle, and Gloria Swanson. Sennett believed he thought better in the bathtub, so he took up to four baths a day. He installed a giant bathtub, five times normal size, next to the desk in his office.

4. BING CROSBY

Bing Crosby was very concerned with his public image. He washed his shirts before sending them to hotel laundries because he was terrified someone might see dirt on his collar.

5. CLARK GABLE

Clark Gable liked to downplay his image as the handsome King of Hollywood. He enjoyed startling guests at parties by popping out his false teeth. Without his dentures, Gable's face would collapse so he was not recognizable as the handsome movie star.

6. ELVIS PRESLEY

By his own admission, Elvis Presley had hundreds of lovers. Women would do almost anything to be near him. Presley had an unusual turn-on: he reportedly liked to watch young women dressed in white panties wrestle.

7. ROSEANNE

Roseanne is known for her outlandish behavior. She offended thousands of people by singing "The Star-Spangled Banner" off-key before a major league baseball game and then grabbing her crotch. One of her most outrageous claims was that she has 27 separate personalities.

8. VIVIEN LEIGH

One way movie stars amused themselves at parties was to play parlor games, which could be cruel. During the filming of *Gone With the Wind,* Vivien Leigh invented a game called "Ways to Kill a Baby."

q. **TUESDAY WELD**

Tuesday Weld created her own open-door policy. Ex-husband Dudley Moore recalled that Weld had the habit of leaving doors open. She would leave cupboard, closet, and even refrigerator doors ajar. She explained her obsession by saying, "I like everything open. I don't like shut doors. I like to see. If I don't see it, it doesn't exist."

10. **WALT DISNEY**

Walt Disney's studio made many classic animated films, including *Snow White and the Seven Dwarfs, Dumbo,* and *Pinocchio.* Disney had an obsession with cleanliness and would wash his hands as often as 30 times an hour.

The One and Only

The 1931 film *Smart Money* was the only movie that co-starred Hollywood's two leading gangster actors, James Cagney and Edward G. Robinson. All of the following are one-of-a-kind Hollywood feats.

1. BARRY FITZGERALD

Barry Fitzgerald is the only person ever to be nominated for an Academy Award for Best Actor and Best Supporting Actor for the same role—portraying a priest in the 1944 film *Going My Way.* Costar Bing Crosby won the Best Actor award, but Fitzgerald won the Oscar for Best Supporting Actor. Because of wartime restrictions, the statue was made of plaster and Fitzgerald accidentally decapitated his Oscar, practicing his golf swing. Paramount Studio spent ten dollars for a replacement.

2. ROLF LESLIE

The only actor to play 27 different roles in a film was Rolf Leslie—in the 1913 film, *Sixty Years as a Queen.*

3. LUPINO LANE

Lupino Lane was literally a one-man show in the appropriately titled *Only Me.* Lane played all 24 roles in the 1929 film.

4. KOLBERG

The record for movie extras in a film was 187,000, used in the 1945 German film *Kolberg.* Joseph Goebbels, in charge of Nazi propaganda, decided to take 187,000 soldiers from battle to appear in the film. Not only did the film not raise public morale in Germany, it deprived the army of much-needed soldiers in the closing months of World War II.

5. *DAYS OF GLORY*

Days of Glory was a 1944 RKO film in which all 19 featured actors were making their movie debut. The only member of the young cast to become a star was Gregory Peck.

6. JAMES DEAN

James Dean, who was killed in an automobile accident in 1955, is the only actor to receive two posthumous Academy Award nominations. Dean was nominated for Best Actor for *East of Eden* in 1955 and *Giant* in 1956, but did not win either year.

7. JANET GAYNOR

Janet Gaynor was the only actress to win one Oscar for three different performances. In 1929, she won the first Best Actress award, in recognition of her performances in *Sunrise, Seventh Heaven,* and *Street Angel.*

8. OSCAR HAMMERSTEIN III

The only person named Oscar to win an Oscar was composer Oscar Hammerstein III. He won Academy Awards for Best Song in 1941 for "The Last Time I Saw Paris" from *Lady Be Good* and four years later for "It Might as Well Be Spring" from the film *State Fair.*

9. GEM THEATER

The Gem Theater was located in Great Yarmouth, England. In 1908, the theater briefly instituted a policy prohibiting men and women from sitting together to discourage inappropriate displays of affection in the theater.

10. LUPE VELEZ

Lupe Velez could do something that no one else in Hollywood could do. The Mexican actress could rotate and counterrotate her left breast. Errol Flynn reportedly was fascinated by this trick.

Believe It or Not

In Hollywood, sometimes fact is stranger than fiction. Michael Keaton had to change his name because his real name was Michael Douglas.

1. WOODY ALLEN

Woody Allen is recognized as one of the world's greatest filmmakers, whose comedy masterpieces include *Manhattan, Annie Hall,* and *Love and Death.* His career as a filmmaker got off to an inauspicious start in 1952 when he dropped out of New York University after failing a film production course.

2. TONYA HARDING

Tonya Harding was a figure skating champion who was banned from the sport in 1994 after pleading guilty to hindering the prosecution in the attack on rival skater Nancy Kerrigan. During the scandal, an X-rated tape of Harding's wedding night with husband Jeff Gillooly was made public. Woody Allen actually offered Harding a role in one of his movies, but, while most actors would give anything to be in a Woody Allen film, Harding turned down the offer because she disapproved of Allen's morals.

3. **CHARLIE CHAPLIN**

During the height of his popularity, Charlie Chaplin was one of the most recognized faces in the world. He once entered a Charlie Chaplin look-alike contest, but, to his amazement, he only finished third.

4. **LAUREN BACALL**

Lauren Bacall is known for her husky voice, but it was decided to dub her voice when she was required to sing a song in the film *To Have and Have Not*. Unable to match the female singer's voice with Bacall's, she was dubbed by a young singer named Andy Williams.

5. **LOU COSTELLO**

Rotund comedian Lou Costello was half of the tremendously successful comedy team Abbott and Costello. Incredibly, Costello began his career in Hollywood as a stunt double for the beautiful actress, Dolores Del Rio.

6. *THE END OF ST. PETERSBURG*

The silent film *The End of St. Petersburg,* released in 1927, dealt with the 1927 Russian revolution. The chamber of commerce in St. Petersburg, Florida, protested release of the film in the United States, however, because it believed the movie would hurt tourism.

7. *THE POPE MUST DIE*

The Pope Must Die was a 1991 film about a plot to kill the Pope and take over the Vatican. The reaction to the title was so negative it was changed to *The Pope Must Diet.*

8. **RONALD REAGAN AND NANCY DAVIS**

In 1949, Nancy Davis was a young actress in Hollywood. It was at the height of the McCarthy era, and Davis was horrified to learn that her name was being circulated on a list of Communist sympathizers in the motion picture industry. Although it turned out to be another actress with the same name, Davis was concerned that the confusion might hinder her career. She contacted Ronald Reagan, president of the Screen Actors Guild at the time, to see if he could help her. They discussed the matter over dinner at the French restaurant La Rue. Later that night, they went to Ciro's to see Sophie Tucker, the Red Hot Mama, perform. Nancy recalled, "I don't know if it was love at first sight, but it was pretty close." The future President and First Lady were married on March 4, 1952.

9. *YPRES*

Cecil B. Demented was John Waters's film about cinema terrorists. In fact, an example of cinematic terrorism did occur in 1925. *Ypres* was a patriotic war film that was targeted by Irish terrorists, who hijacked the film from a Dublin theater at gunpoint. When the theater got another print and attempted to show the film, it was blown up.

10. **MARY PICKFORD**

Mary Pickford was known as The Girl with the Curls. Pickford's hair was short, so she had to wear false curls in the movies. The golden curls worn by America's Sweetheart were actually cut from the hair of prostitutes from Suzy's French Whorehouse in Los Angeles.

Outrageous Actors

Hollywood has had its share of outrageous personalities. It seems as if Madonna will do almost anything to get attention. Pamela Anderson had "Tommy" tattooed on her finger when she wed rocker Tommy Lee. When they divorced, Anderson had the tattoo changed to read "Mommy." Some actors refuse to be ignored.

1. TALLULAH BANKHEAD

Tallulah Bankhead was known more for her sharp wit than for her film career. "I detest acting because it's sheer drudgery," she admitted. She said her main reason for going to Hollywood was "to fuck that divine Gary Cooper." Bankhead claimed to have had more than 5,000 lovers, male and female. "I'm as pure as the driven slush," Tallulah quipped. She told Ginger Rogers, "Any husband of yours is a husband of mine," and she shocked Joan Crawford by telling her, "I've had an affair with your husband [Douglas Fairbanks Jr.]. You'll be next."

At a society wedding Tallulah boasted, "I've had both of them, darling, and neither of them is any good." At parties, she would stand on her head to show everyone she didn't wear panties. Once she dove into a swimming pool while dressed in an evening gown and wearing expensive jewelry. In the pool she did a striptease until she was nude. "Everybody's been dying to see my body," she explained. When she learned Marlene Dietrich sprinkled gold dust in her hair, Bankhead said she sprinkled gold dust in her pubic hair. Tallulah argued that cocaine was not habit-forming: "Of course, cocaine isn't habit-forming, and I should know. I've been using it for 20 years." When someone tried to match wits with Bankhead, he or she usually came out on the short end. When columnist Earl Wilson asked, "Have you ever been mistaken for a man?" Tallulah replied, "No darling, have you?" Howard Dietz said of her, "A day away from Tallulah is like a month in the country."

2. W. C. FIELDS

W. C. Fields's pronouncements included, "I'm free of prejudice. I hate everybody equally," and "Anyone who hates small dogs and children can't be all bad." He once spiked Baby LeRoy's milk with gin, and, when the inebriated child was unable to perform, Fields said, "The kid's no trouper." Known for his own prodigious drinking, Fields pretended to drink fruit juice on the set when he was really drinking gin. In a vain attempt to keep Fields sober during filming, someone actually put fruit juice into the container. On drinking from the container, Fields spit it out, exclaiming, "Some son of a bitch put pineapple juice in my pineapple juice." "Once during Prohibition," he announced on another occasion, "I was forced to live for days on nothing but food and water." Asked what he would do differently if he could live his life again, Fields said, "I'd live over a saloon."

To conceal his assets from the Internal Revenue Service, Fields had secret bank accounts throughout the country under such outrageous names as Primrose Magoo, Mahatma Kane Jeeves, and Felton J. Satchelstern. During World War II, he even had an account in Germany "in case that little bastard wins." On his deathbed, Fields was seen reading the Bible. "I'm looking for loopholes," he explained.

3. JOHN BARRYMORE

Douglas Fairbanks Jr. said of John Barrymore, "He is reported to have witnessed and indulged in every known vice." According to Barrymore, "The good die young because they see it's no use living if you've got to be good." Once unable to get an alcoholic drink, Barrymore gulped down his wife's perfume. On another occasion, he stumbled into the ladies' bathroom, where a producer's wife discovered him urinating. She scolded him, saying, "Mr. Barrymore, this is for ladies." Barrymore turned around and showed her his penis. "So, madam, is this," he said. When Barrymore saw a very elderly man in a cemetery at a funeral, the actor said, "It's hardly worth going home." At an auction held to liquidate Barrymore's estate upon his death in 1942, Edgar Bergen paid $185 for Barrymore's collection of Ecuadorian shrunken heads, and Barrymore's girdle sold for $4.50.

4. MAE WEST

Mae West said she lost her virginity at age 12 when she was ravished by a bear in a dream. She next year she had her first human lover, her music teacher, with whom she made love on the steps of her parents' home. When Hedda Hopper asked West how she learned so much about men, Mae replied, "I went to night school." West was especially fond of male bodybuilders. "A hard man is good to find," Mae explained. Another of her typical sayings was, "To err is human, but it feels divine."

The quintessential Mae West quote, however, was: "When I'm good, I'm very good. But when I'm bad, I'm better." In her films, she sometimes wore gowns so tight she couldn't move and would be propped up on a reclining board between takes. West was so proud of her breasts she occasionally took them out to allow someone to admire their size and firmness. In 1985, when the 82-year-old West acted in her final film, *Sextette,* she was so feeble she was fed her lines through an earpiece. During shooting, a traffic helicopter passed overhead on the same frequency, and, in the middle of the scene, West began reciting the traffic report.

5. **ZSA ZSA GABOR**

Zsa Zsa Gabor appeared in a few good films, such as *Moulin Rouge* (1952) and *Touch of Evil,* and lots of bad films, such as *Queen of Outer Space* and *Pepe.* Zsa Zsa's love life overshadowed her movie career, however. She rated her lovers on a scale of 1 (worst) to 10 (best). Frank Sinatra was given a 1; Sean Connery received a perfect 10. According to Gabor, "The best way to attract a man immediately is to have a magnificent bosom and a half-sized brain and let both of them show." The oft-married actress said, "Darling, I'm a marvelous housekeeper; every time I divorce a man, I keep the house."

6. **OSCAR LEVANT**

Oscar Levant said of Zsa Zsa Gabor, "She's discovered the secret of perpetual middle age." A concert pianist and renowned wit, Levant starred in some of Hollywood's best musicals, including *The Band Wagon* and *An American in Paris.* He once observed, "Strip the phony tinsel off Hollywood, and you'll find the real tinsel underneath." A notorious hypochondriac, Levant joked, "I don't drink, it makes me feel good."

7. SHIRLEY MACLAINE

Yves Montand said of Shirley MacLaine, "Who does she think she isn't?" Shirley MacLaine believes in reincarnation and claims to have had many past lives, among them a Mongolian nomad, a Parisian dance hall girl, and a court jester who was beheaded by King Louis XV.

8. MERCEDES McCAMBRIDGE

Mercedes McCambridge won an Academy Award in 1949 for her supporting performance in *All the King's Men.* She was especially good at playing sexually frustrated women in films such as *Lighting Strikes Twice* and *Johnny Guitar.* When McCambridge was selected to provide the voice of the devil in *The Exorcist,* she used some unconventional techniques to create demonic sounds. She swallowed 18 raw eggs and a pulpy apple to produce the unforgettable sound of the possessed girl spewing out green vomit, and she pulled a scarf tightly around her neck to create the groaning sounds. The part, for which she was not credited on-screen, was so strenuous it took her months to recover from filming.

9. DENNIS HOPPER

Tuesday Weld said of Dennis Hopper, "I think he has a dilating brain." Hopper's portrayal of psychotic killer Frank Booth in *Blue Velvet* is one of the most chilling in film history. Hopper even said of himself, "I'm just a hair away from being a serial killer." He went through a period of substance abuse that resulted in aberrant behavior, admitting, "I was doing half an ounce of cocaine every three days. I was drinking half a gallon of rum a day with 28 beers." In April 1983, Hopper, hallucinating from drugs, was found walking naked on a road in Mexico after being fired from the film *Jungle Warriors.*

10. **GRETA GARBO**

Greta Garbo considered her privacy more important than her film career. Robert Montgomery said of her, "Making a film with Garbo does not constitute an introduction." Garbo claimed of Hollywood, "This is where I wasted the best years of my life." The woman who said, "I want to be left alone," retired from films in 1942 and spent the last 48 years of her life guarding her privacy. Publicist Howard Dietz asked Garbo to have dinner on a particular Monday night, but Garbo declined, saying, "How do you know I'll be hungry on Monday?"

Outrageous Directors

The director is the single most important person in the making of a film, and each of these directors had his own unique approach to making movies.

1. JOHN WATERS

John Waters is the master of bad taste. His credo is, "Bad taste is what entertainment is all about." His first film, a 15-minute short, entitled *Hag in a Black Leather Jacket*, was about the wedding ceremony of a black man and a white woman performed by a Ku Klux Klansman. The star of many of his films was Divine, a 300-pound bald actor in drag, whose real name was Harris Glenn Milstead. Waters's *Mondo Trasho* (1969) starred Divine as a woman who was confined to a mental institution after witnessing a miracle in a launderette. His next film, *Multiple Maniacs*, featured a scene in which Divine was raped by a giant lobster. Waters's masterpiece of bad taste, *Pink Flamingos*, was released in 1972. The plot concerned a competition to discover the most disgusting person on Earth. For the past 30 years, Waters has continued to explore the underside of American culture in such films as *Female Trouble, Desperate Living, Polyester,* and *Pecker.*

2. ERICH VON STROHEIM

Erich von Stroheim directed several silent film classics, including *The Merry Widow, The Wedding March,* and *Greed.* His films were lavish productions that went way over budget, and he insisted on absolute realism, sometimes to ridiculous extremes. In *The Merry-Go-Round,* Stroheim insisted the actors playing royal guardsmen wear silk underpants monogrammed with the emblem of Austria's Imperial Guard, even though viewers would not see them. Stroheim argued that the authentic underclothes would motivate the actors to give better performances. He also used real streetwalkers to play prostitutes in *The Wedding March.* The director tried to release *Greed* as a nine-hour film and was outraged when the studio cut nearly seven hours of it. His films often featured orgies and other forms of decadence, and he was known as "The Man You Love to Hate." Actress Mae Murray called Stroheim "The Dirty Hun." Stroheim's extravagance was too much for the studios, and he directed his last film in 1928; however, he did act in films after that, most notably in *Sunset Boulevard.*

3. HENRY JAGLOM

Independent director Henry Jaglom has made a series of highly personal films. His directorial debut in 1971, *A Safe Place,* starred Jack Nicholson, Tuesday Weld, and Orson Welles. The intriguing fantasy was described by Jaglom as an "essay on time and memory." Jaglom's methods of getting actors to give the performances he wanted were unconventional; he could be incredibly generous or openly confrontational. Jaglom doesn't hesitate to whip an actor into a frenzy to reach the "truth" the director is seeking. Jaglom's goal was to capture a piece of time with his actors. According to one actress who worked with him, "By the end of the day you want to shoot yourself." Jaglom's brother, actor Michael Emil, said, "It's amazing that he hasn't been beaten up several times because of the way he treats people." Jaglom puts his actors under pressure to discover their weaknesses, then pushes the right buttons to get them to shed their inhibitions. He has been known also for his unique fashion sense. Candice Bergen described Jaglom, in the 1970s, as looking like a "samurai transvestite." Much of the dialogue in Jaglom's films is improvised and the productions have almost a home movie look. Some of Jaglom's most interesting films include *Sitting Ducks, Can She Bake a Cherry Pie?, Always,* and *New Year's Day.*

4. **ALFRED HITCHCOCK**

Alfred Hitchcock's films often displayed black humor. In real life, the director enjoyed shocking his actors with his warped sense of humor. During the filming of *Psycho,* Hitchcock had tea every afternoon at 4 P.M., and he insisted on having the skeletal Mrs. Bates seated at the table. He delighted in introducing Anthony Perkins, the actor who played Norman Bates, as Master Bates. Hitchcock once threw a dinner party at which all the food was dyed blue.

One of his cruelest practical jokes was played on an unfortunate member of the crew. Hitch bet the cameraman the latter couldn't spend a night in a dark studio. The man was handcuffed to his chair, then Hitchcock gave him a bottle of brandy to calm his nerves. What he didn't tell the man was that the brandy was laced with laxatives. Hitchcock once referred to actors as cattle. While filming *Mr. and Mrs. Smith,* Carole Lombard, a notorious practical joker, brought three heifers onto the set. According to Hitchcock, "Walt Disney, of course, has the best casting. If he doesn't like an actor, he just tears him up."

5. **CECIL B. DE MILLE**

Cecil B. De Mille is best known for his Biblical epics, such as *King of Kings* and *The Ten Commandments*. De Mille had the stars of *King of Kings* sign contracts promising their future behavior would not detract from their religious screen personas. De Mille got away with murder because of the Biblical subject matter: he filmed orgy scenes, nude women, women kissing women, and unspeakable violence. If a critic objected to one of his films, De Mille replied, "If you condemn my Bible pictures, you condemn the Bible." In 1934, De Mille sent art director Cameron Menzies to Egypt at a cost of $100,000 to visit all 92 pyramids. The purpose of the trip was to find out their true color. Menzies reported the pyramids were a sandy brown. However, after going to the trouble and expense to learn the color of the pyramids, De Mille shot *Cleopatra* in black and white.

6. **OTTO PREMINGER**

Otto Preminger directed film classics such as *Laura* and *Anatomy of a Murder.* His relationships with actors were not always cordial. For example, Dyan Cannon called him a "horrible man"; Michael Caine said of him, "Otto Preminger is only happy if everyone else is miserable"; Joan Crawford described him as a "Jewish Nazi"; and Jean Seberg, whom Preminger discovered and made into a star in *Saint Joan,* vowed that she "hated his guts." Director Billy Wilder claimed Preminger was "really Martin Bormann in elevator shoes with a face-lift by a blindfolded plastic surgeon." After Jackie

Gleason saw Preminger chew out an elderly Groucho Marx, he warned the director, "If you ever talk to me like that, I'll hit you over the head with a fucking chair." While filming *Exodus,* Preminger brought some child actors to tears by screaming, "Cry, you little monsters!" He compared critics to eunuchs because "they can watch, but cannot perform." A favorite target of his was Marilyn Monroe, whom he described as a "vacuum with nipples." Monroe had a fantasy of having a child with Albert Einstein; she once speculated the child would be perfect if it had her looks and his brains. Preminger speculated, "What if the child had Einstein's looks and Marilyn's brain?"

7. HENRY HATHAWAY

Henry Hathaway's rapport with actors was just about as good as Otto Preminger's. Hathaway intimidated his actors, sometimes to the verge of a nervous breakdown. Richard Widmark, who gave a brilliant performance as psychotic killer Tommy Udo in Hathaway's *Kiss of Death,* attributed his character's famous giggle to the actor being unnerved by the director. In the 1958 film *From Hell to Texas,* it took Dennis Hopper 86 takes to film a scene. Hathaway told the young actor, "You'll never work in this town again." Hopper didn't appear in a major Hollywood film for another seven years, when Hathaway hired him for *The Sons of Katie Elder.*

8. ANDY WARHOL

Pop artist Andy Warhol directed dozens of films between 1963 and 1973, with titles such as *Blow Job, Taylor Mead's Ass,* and *Eating Too Fast.* Other films had one-word titles—*Kiss, Eat, Sleep, Haircut, Face,* and *Drunk.* As the titles suggest, Warhol would point a camera at a sometimes stationary object for hours. The actors in Warhol's films were usually members of his entourage, drag queens, and "superstars" he created.

9. CHARLIE CHAPLIN

Charlie Chaplin was one of cinema's greatest comic geniuses. A perfectionist, he filmed a record 342 takes of the touching final scene of *City Lights* between The Little Tramp and the blind girl whose sight has been restored. In *City Lights,* Chaplin had wife Paulette Goddard portray a scrubwoman. To get her into character, he asked Goddard to scrub the entire set; she refused and walked off the set. Edna Purviance, a favorite actress of Chaplin's, appeared in many of his early films. Although she retired in 1926, Chaplin kept her on contract at full salary until her death 32 years later.

10. VICTOR FLEMING

In 1939 Victor Fleming directed two classics of American cinema, *The Wizard of Oz* and *Gone With the Wind.* Fleming was reputed to be a tough guy and a ladies' man, and he was not afraid to abuse an actress physically to get the desired response. Ingrid Bergman recalled Fleming slapping her because the scene required her to be hysterical. Judy Garland also felt the back of his hand, and he once twisted Lana Turner's arm to make her cry.

Cult Actors

Some actors have their own cult followings. They appear in cult movies, and their devotees regard them with a special reverence. They may not be the biggest stars, but they probably have the most devoted followings.

1. DIVINE

Divine said, "My life is a drag, thank goodness." The cross-dressing actor proved to be the muse of director John Waters. Divine gladly subjected himself to every possible indignity to bring Waters's twisted vision of America to the screen. Two of Divine's most memorable creations were the disgusting Babs Johnson in *Pink Flamingos* and Tab Hunter's lover, Francine Fishpaw, in *Polyester.*

2. TOR JOHNSON

Tor Johnson was a 400-pound wrestler known as the Swedish Angel before he was discovered by bad film director extraordinaire Ed Wood. Although Johnson could barely speak English and had virtually no acting ability, he was featured in a number of Wood's most memorable movies: *Bride of the Monster, Plan 9 from Outer Space,* and *The Night of the Ghouls.* Wood hated inviting Johnson to his home because he invariably broke the toilet seats in the director's home with his great weight.

3. LISA MARIE

Curvaceous actress Lisa Marie, the companion of director Tim Burton for a number of years, appeared in a number of Burton films, often in an eye-catching, unusual role. She played Vampira in *Ed Wood;* she was the alien disguised as a woman, who bites off Martin Short's finger in *Mars Attacks;* and she played an ape in Burton's *Planet of the Apes.*

4. BUD CORT

Bud Cort has been a cult movie fan favorite since his role as a boy who wants to fly like a bird in Robert Altman's 1970 film, *Brewster McCloud.* His most celebrated role, however, was that of a young man obsessed with suicide in the cult movie favorite *Harold and Maude.* Cort excels at playing gentle characters, such as a man who befriends Nastassja Kinski in *Maria's Lovers* and an art expert in *Pollock.*

5. EDITH MASSEY

Edith Massey held the distinction of being the most grotesque actress in John Waters's repertory company. Massey was ugly, nearly toothless, and obese, with an especially irritating voice. She played the Egg Lady in *Pink Flamingos,* and, in *Female Trouble,* she portrayed Aunt Ida, who tosses acid in Divine's face. She also played the despicable Queen Carlotta in *Desperate Living,* who injects her daughter with rabies.

6. CRISWELL

Criswell was a newscaster who discovered he could make a better living as a crackpot psychic. A regular guest on *The Tonight Show*, Criswell had memorable but few film roles. As the narrator in *Plan 9 from Outer Space,* he asks the incredulous viewers, "Can you prove it didn't happen?" He rose from a coffin in Wood's *Night of the Ghouls* to serve once again as a narrator. Criswell played the Emperor of the Dead in the soft-porn graveyard flick, *Orgy of the Dead,* also written by Wood.

7. RONDO HATTON

Rondo Hatton suffered from acromegaly, a condition that left him with a misshapen head. The studios shamelessly billed him as the Ugliest Man in Pictures and cast him in a series of horror movies, in which he played freaks, killers, and monsters. His most memorable performance was as the Creeper in *Pearl of Death.*

8. TURA SATANA

Tura Satana was unforgettable as the voluptuous killing machine in Russ Meyer's *Faster, Pussycat! Kill! Kill!* Her karate skills came in handy when she played a CIA assassin in the 1973 film *Doll Squad.* She also starred in the bad film classic *The Astro Zombies.*

9. DYANNE THORNE

Sexy blonde Dyanne Thorne played a seductive camp commandant in *Ilsa, She-Wolf of the SS.* Thorne continued her brutality in the sequel, *Ilsa, Harem Keeper of the Oil Sheiks,* and she was back with her evil ways a few years later in *Ilsa, the Wicked Warden.* Thorne also starred in *The Erotic Adventures of Pinocchio,* a film in which his nose is not the part of Pinocchio's anatomy that grows.

10. **MICHAEL EMIL**

Michael Emil has starred in several of his brother, Henry Jaglom's, films. His specialty was playing characters who constantly talk about their strange views on the effects of sex on their lives. Emil was especially good in *Sitting Ducks,* in which he costars with Zack Norman as a pair of schemers on the run from the Mafia. Emil's best-known role was as an Albert Einstein–inspired character in *Insignificance.*

Outrageous Movies

Some films have outrageous concepts, offbeat performances, and offensive material. These films had something to offend everyone.

1. *PINK FLAMINGOS*

The 1972 film *Pink Flamingos,* directed by John Waters, had as its premise a competition to determine who was the filthiest person on Earth. Some of the despicable acts the characters perform include cannibalism, baby brokering, and selling heroin to elementary school children. Babs Johnson, played by Divine, proves she's the filthiest of all by eating dog excrement. What made the scene even more disgusting was that Divine actually did eat dog poop.

2. *THE WORM EATERS*

The 1977 film *The Worm Eaters* told the story of a worm breeder who turns people into squirming wormlike creatures by putting nightcrawlers in their food. Star Herb Robins helped to promote the film by going to theaters and demonstrating his worm-eating technique. Free admission was offered to anyone who would eat a worm.

3. *SNUFF*

Snuff caused a sensation when it was released in the mid-1970s. It's a dull movie about an Argentine drug-smuggling ring, but what made the film controversial was the rumor that an actress who is stabbed to death in the final scene actually was killed. When it was revealed that it was not really a snuff film, interest in it quickly waned.

4. *THE TERROR OF TINY TOWN*

The Terror of Tiny Town was the first and last western with an all-midget cast; the cowboys all rode low on the saddle on Shetland ponies. Billy Curtis, who played the hero in *The Terror of Tiny Town,* appeared the next year as the Lord High Mayor, a munchkin, in *The Wizard of Oz.*

5. *THE CURE FOR INSOMNIA*

The Cure for Insomnia was a 1987 film directed by John Henry Timmis IV. The film lasted 85 hours, much of which was spent reading a 4,080-page poem entitled *The Cure for Insomnia.*

6. *BATHROOM INTIMACIES*

Bathroom Intimacies was a 1990 Mexican film that recorded the bowel movements of a family. Incredibly, this was not the first film about going to the bathroom. In 1912, a Hungarian film, *Bitter Love,* dealt entirely with people going to the bathroom as the result of an intestinal virus caused by contaminated water.

7. *HAPPY END*

Happy End was a 1968 Czech film in which all the action is shown from the end to the beginning. People walk back-

ward, and answers precede questions. In one scene, a guil-
lotined head is reattached to its body.

8. *THE ANNUNCIATION*

The Annunciation was a 1984 Hungarian film, whose cast
was made up entirely of children. The story portrays Adam
guided through history, and Satan was played by a nine-
year-old girl.

9. *DEAFULA*

There have been many parodies of *Dracula,* from *Blackula,*
featuring a black vampire, to the soft-core porn film, *Spermula,*
which has nothing to do with blood sucking. *Deafula* is Dracula's hearing-impaired illegitimate son, and the 1975 film
was done entirely in sign language.

10. *ERASERHEAD*

Director David Lynch's first feature film, *Eraserhead,* is unlike
any movie you'll ever see. The main character of the 1978
cult classic, a dark nightmare of a film, is Henry Spencer,
played by John Nance with a hairstyle only Don King would
love. The scene in which Henry meets his girlfriend's parents
can be described best as surreal. His girlfriend is spastic, and
her parents are insane. Henry is served a small chicken that
moves when he tries to carve it, and the film ends with
Henry sitting in his apartment attempting to care for his
mutant baby.

Incredibly Strange Titles

S ome films are more notable for their titles than for their content. *Cottonpickin' Chickenpickers, I Eat Your Skin* and *Mars Needs Women* are just a few of them.

1. *THE INCREDIBLY STRANGE CREATURES WHO STOPPED LIVING AND BECAME MIXED-UP ZOMBIES*

The Incredibly Strange Creatures Who Stopped Living and Became Mixed-Up Zombies, directed by Ray Dennis Steckler, was billed as Hollywood's first monster musical. One of the songs was titled "The Mixed-Up Zombie Stomp," and the plot concerned a gypsy fortune-teller who creates a race of hideous zombies by throwing acid into their faces. The film's alternate title was the shorter *The Teenage Psycho Meets Bloody Mary.*

2. *RAT PFINK A BOO BOO*

Rat Pfink a Boo Boo was another film directed by Ray Dennis Steckler. Made in 1966, it was an obvious attempt to capitalize on the success of the campy television series *Batman.* It dealt with a not-so-superhero and his boy wonder. The title was supposed to be *Rat Pfink and Boo Boo,* but when the credits were printed *Rat Pfink a Boo Boo* mistakenly, Steckler didn't have the money to correct it.

3. *JESSE JAMES MEETS FRANKENSTEIN'S DAUGHTER*

Director William Beaudine decided it was a great idea to mix two movie genres, westerns and horror films, in *Jesse James Meets Frankenstein's Daughter.* The title was not really accurate; the character in the film was actually Dr. Frankenstein's granddaughter. Beaudine also directed the equally awful *Billy the Kid vs. Dracula.*

4. *BELA LUGOSI MEETS A BROOKLYN GORILLA*

Bela Lugosi began his slide into terrible films when he starred in the 1952 turkey *Bela Lugosi Meets a Brooklyn Gorilla.* Lugosi plays a mad scientist who meets two men from Brooklyn: Duke Mitchell and Sammy Petrillo, who were imitations of the popular comedy team of Martin and Lewis.

5. *THE RATS ARE COMING! THE WEREWOLVES ARE HERE*

The 1972 film *The Rats Are Coming! The Werewolves Are Here* tells the story of a family of werewolves that raised man-eating rats. In an attempt to get rid of the rats featured in the film, the producer held prize drawings to give a free rat to anyone who promised to give it to his or her mother-in-law.

6. *I DISMEMBER MAMA*

For *I Dismember Mama,* a 1972 slasher film, viewers were offered an upchuck cup in case the gore made them ill. The director, Paul Leder, made another film, entitled *Please Don't Eat My Mother.*

7. *CHILDREN SHOULDN'T PLAY WITH DEAD THINGS*

Children Shouldn't Play with Dead Things was a 1970 zombie film that combined comedy and horror. The film's director, Bob Clark, later directed a critically panned but commercially successful comedy, *Porky's,* as well as the beloved holiday comedy *A Christmas Story.*

8. *SANTA CLAUS CONQUERS THE MARTIANS*

Santa Claus Conquers the Martians was unleashed on unsuspecting children in 1964. Santa is kidnapped by Martians, including a particularly annoying alien named Dropo. The film marked the movie debut of Pia Zadora. In 1982, a grown-up Zadora was the controversial choice as Best New Star at the Golden Globe Awards.

9. *SURF NAZIS MUST DIE*

Over the years, there have been many bad films made about surfers and about Nazis. *Surf Nazis Must Die,* a 1987 film about a gang that controlled a Los Angeles beach, combined them.

10. *NIGHT OF THE DAY OF THE DAWN OF THE SON OF THE BRIDE OF THE RETURN OF THE REVENGE OF THE TERROR OF THE ATTACK OF THE EVIL MUTANT HELL-BOUND ZOMBIEFIED FLESH-EATING SUB-HUMANOID LIVING DEAD—PART 4*

If ever a title said it all, it was the 1993 film, *Night of the Day of the Dawn of the Son of the Bride of the Return of the Revenge of the Terror of the Attack of the Evil Mutant Hellbound Zombiefied Flesh-Eating Sub-Humanoid Living Dead—Part 4.* The title parodied the entire horror genre, from zombie flicks to monster movie sequels.

You Got to Have a Gimmick

The first feature film done in 3-D was a 1936 Italian movie *Nozze Vagabonde*. The 3-D craze swept America in the early 1950s in such films as *Bwana Devil* and *House of Wax*. Since then, moviemakers have come up with all kinds of gimmicks to lure people into the theater. Producers of the 1982 film *Hitler* had Adolf Hitler look-alike contests and gave free passes to the winners. Roger Corman required patrons to take a mental health test before viewing his horror film *Dementia 13*, and, for his 1982 film *Polyester*, John Waters gave moviegoers scratch-and-sniff cards to be used at various times in the movie. He called the process Odorama.

1. EMERGO

William Castle was the master of promotional gimmicks. The producer-director had a different gimmick for each of his horror films. His 1959 film, *House on Haunted Hill*, featured Vincent Price as a man who offered $50,000 to anyone who would spend the night in his haunted house. Castle devised a shock for the film named Emergo. Emergo was an inflatable skeleton suspended above the audience. Although the flying luminous skeletons were intended to scare the audience, most moviegoers laughed at them, and many kids brought slingshots to shoot at them.

2. **PERCEPTO**

Another Castle creation was Percepto, the gimmick for his film *The Tingler*. The Tingler was a creature that squeezed the spines of terrified people, and the only way to stop him was to scream. Castle rigged certain seats in the theater so their occupants would get an electric shock.

3. **SMELL-O-VISION**

Smell-O-Vision was the promotional idea Mike Todd Jr., used for his 1960 film, *The Scent of Mystery*. It was billed as the first movie to "stink on purpose." During the film, 52 different scents were released through vents into the theater. Among the odors were perfume, wine, tobacco, garlic, wood shavings, and gunpowder. Comedian Henny Youngman joked, "I didn't understand the film. I had a cold." The concept did not catch on, and the film was rereleased without the scents under a new title, *Holiday in Spain*.

4. *MOM and DAD*

Mom and Dad was a 1947 film that featured a childbirth scene. Nauseating chemicals were piped through the ventilation system during the childbirth scene, causing moviegoers to run gagging from the theater.

5. **PUNISHMENT POLL**

Mr. Sardonicus was a William Castle film about a homicidal maniac whose face was frozen in a grotesque grin. Near the end of the movie, the film was stopped, and the audience was asked to decide Mr. Sardonicus's fate by holding up fluorescent thumb cards. Thumbs up, he lived; thumbs down, he died. The audience always chose death, which was lucky for Castle, because he had filmed just one ending.

6. *CRIMINALLY INSANE*

Criminally Insane was a horror film about Fat Ethel, a 250-pound cannibal who chopped up her victims with a meat cleaver. In a tasteless promotion, any woman who weighed in at more than 200 pounds was admitted free.

7. **BURIAL INSURANCE**

The Night of a Thousand Cats was a film about man-eating cats. The filmmakers ran ads that offered burial insurance to anyone who died of fright while viewing the film, but, fortunately, no one needed to claim the benefit.

8. **GHOST VIEWER**

An ingenious William Castle gimmick was the ghost viewer he devised for his film *13 Ghosts.* He filmed the movie in the Illusion-O process: each person in the audience was equipped with red and blue tinted glasses. If you looked through the red strip, you would see the ghost; anyone looking through the blue strip could remove the ghost.

9. **HALLUCINOGENIC HYPNOVISION**

At one point in *The Incredibly Strange Creatures Who Stopped Living and Became Crazy Mixed-Up Zombies,* a spiraling hypnotic wheel was shown on the screen. This was the signal for ushers wearing glowing bloody masks and carrying cardboard axes to run up the aisles. Some of the ushers were attacked by hysterical audience members.

10. FEAR FLASHER AND HORROR HORN

Producer Hy Averback had two gimmicks for his 1966 film, *Chamber of Horrors*. The film was about a deranged killer loose in a wax museum. Whenever a frightening moment was about to occur, a loud horn, called the Horror Horn, was sounded, and a red flashing light, called the Fear Flasher, was shown. The warning gave moviegoers a chance to close their eyes.

Movie Mistakes

Occasionally things end up in films that are not intended. In *Abbott and Costello Meet the Mummy,* the comedy team refer to each other by their real names, Bud and Lou, instead of their characters' names, Pete and Freddie. In *Jaws, the Revenge,* Michael Caine dives into the water and climbs out perfectly dry. In the famed chase scene in *Bullitt,* the car Steve McQueen drives loses six hubcaps. The title of the film, *Krakatoa, East of Java,* is inaccurate since the volcano was actually located 200 miles west of Java. The 1961 prison film *Seven Women from Hell* had in fact only six females in the cast. In the film *Abbott and Costello Go to Mars,* the comedy team actually goes to Venus.

1. *THE CRUSADES*

In the 1935 Cecil B. De Mille epic, *The Crusades,* a king pulls back his cape and looks at his wristwatch. Apparently De Mille didn't learn from the gaffe, however; 21 years later, in *The Ten Commandments,* a blind man is wearing a wristwatch.

2. *anaTOMy OF a MURDER*

Anatomy of a Murder was a nominee for Best Picture at the 1959 Academy Awards. The film did include one blatant mistake: actress Lee Remick walks out of a café wearing a long flowing skirt. When she comes through the door on the other side, however, she's wearing slacks.

3. *EL CID*

El Cid, a 1961 film starring Charlton Heston and Sophia Loren, is supposed to be set in the eleventh century. Someone forgot to tell one of the extras, who is wearing sunglasses.

4. *aBE LINcoln In ILLINoIS*

There's a scene in *Abe Lincoln in Illinois* where Lincoln, played by Raymond Massey, is on a train about to take him from his home in Illinois to Washington, D.C. One of the wellwishers can be heard to say, "Goodbye, Mr. Massey."

5. *BODy DOUBLE*

In the 1984 film *Body Double,* Melanie Griffith played porn star Holly Body. During the filming of an adult movie scene, the reflection of the camera crew can be seen clearly in the mirror.

6. *THE WRONG BOX*

The 1966 film *The Wrong Box* was set in Victorian England, but in one scene, television antennas can be seen on the tops of some of the buildings.

7. *REaR WINDOW*

Even a director as great as Alfred Hitchcock can make a mistake. *Rear Window* is a 1954 classic about a photographer, played by James Stewart, who is confined to his room with a broken leg. In one scene in the film, Stewart's cast switches from his left leg to his right leg.

8. *GONE WITH THE WIND*

The Civil War epic *Gone With the Wind* won the 1939 Academy Award for Best Picture, but the film does contain a major flub. As Scarlett O'Hara, played by Vivien Leigh, walks down the street in Atlanta, she passes an electric street lamp.

9. *THE SOUND OF MUSIC*

The Sound of Music was set in the 1930s. However, sharp-eyed viewers may spot a crate of oranges that has "Product of Israel" written on it. Israel didn't come into existence as a nation until after World War II.

10. *DECAMERON NIGHTS*

Decameron Nights, a 1953 film starring Louis Jourdan, is set in the fourteenth century. During a shot of a pirate ship, an anachronistic white truck can be seen driving on land in the background.

Film Flops

Today, movies can cost as much as $200 million to make, sometimes causing producers to lose tens of millions of dollars on a commercial bomb. Some films lose so much money they can actually sink a studio. Each of these 10 films was a box office disaster.

1. *HEAVEN'S GATE*

Heaven's Gate was director Michael Cimino's follow-up to his critically acclaimed film *The Deer Hunter.* Cimino hoped that *Heaven's Gate* would be his masterpiece. The original budget soared from $7 million to $57 million for a number of reasons. For example, to create the effect he wanted, Cimino covered an area of grassland with brown and yellow paint. There were endless retakes, and a record 220 hours of film was shot for the $3^1/_2$-hour movie. Sadly, audiences booed the film at its Hollywood premiere in April 1981. When the costs of filming and distribution were factored in, *Heaven's Gate* reportedly lost nearly $100 million.

2. *ISHTAR*

Released in 1987, *Ishtar* was an ill-advised attempt to make a comedy team out of Warren Beatty and Dustin Hoffman. They were cast as a pair of singer-songwriters, but neither could sing, and the film wasn't funny. In an interview, Hoffman invited the public to "come and see the end of two careers." *Ishtar* lost nearly $50 million.

3. *HUDSON HAWK*

Not even Bruce Willis's considerable box office appeal could save the 1991 debacle, *Hudson Hawk*. Willis portrayed a cat burglar trying to retrieve a part for a machine that could turn lead to gold. The film was universally panned, and, according to *People* magazine, "This is the movie playing all the time on every screen of every theater in Hell." The film, which cost $65 million to make, earned only $8 million.

4. *THE SWARM*

The Swarm was a 1978 film about a swarm of African killer bees unleashed in the southwestern United States, directed by Irwin Allen, who was known for his disaster films, *The Poseidon Adventure* and *The Towering Inferno*. The all-star cast included Henry Fonda, Michael Caine, Richard Widmark, and Katharine Ross. Actor George Kennedy described *The Swarm* as "a disaster as a disaster movie." Critic Alan Brien claimed it was "simply the worst film ever made."

5. *CUTTHROAT ISLAND*

Cutthroat Island was one of the costliest flops in film history. The 1995 film, which starred Geena Davis and Matthew

Modine, about a woman who scalps her dying father and discovers a treasure map tattooed on the top of his head, was no treasure at the box office and lost more than $80 million.

6. *THE ADVENTURES OF BARON MUNCHAUSEN*

The Adventures of Baron Munchausen, a 1989 film directed by Monty Python member Terry Gilliam, was the story of Baron Munchausen, who told tall tales about his life. Apparently, the movie public didn't believe it; the film lost nearly $50 million.

7. *SGT. PEPPER'S LONELY HEARTS CLUB BAND*

Sgt. Pepper's Lonely Hearts Club Band is the Beatles record frequently called the greatest rock album ever made. In 1978, rock impresario Robert Stigwood decided to make a film of the same name featuring 29 Beatles songs. Rock stars Peter Frampton and the Bee Gees were recruited to play the band. The film was a mess, however, and a critical and box office disaster.

8. *1941*

1941 was proof that even Steven Spielberg could make a box office bomb. The director of *Jaws* and *Close Encounters of the Third Kind* tried his hand at comedy with a film about a Japanese attack on Los Angeles in 1941. It proved to be about as funny as Pearl Harbor: the $40-million film starring John Belushi was a critical and box office failure.

9. *INCHON*

Inchon was a big-budget 1982 film about a crucial battle in the Korean War. Film critic Vincent Canby called it "The most expensive B movie ever made." The picture lost nearly $50 million.

10. *PIRATES*

Pirates was a 1986 film starring Walter Matthau and directed by Roman Polanski. Polanski spent $10 million on a full-scale replica of a Spanish galleon, but the film sank at the box office without a trace.

The Worst Movies Ever Made

They Saved Hitler's Brain was a 1963 film about a group of fanatics who try to take over the world by following orders from Adolf Hitler's severed head. *Attack of the Killer Tomatoes* was a 1978 film about giant man-eating tomatoes. The 1938 film *Reefer Madness* ridiculously attempted to depict the evils of smoking marijuana. Some films are so bad they're actually fun to watch.

1. *PLAN 9 FROM OUTER SPACE*

Plan 9 from Outer Space has been called the *Citizen Kane* of bad films. Early in the film, narrator Criswell says, "There comes a time in every man's life when he just can't believe his eyes." The statement sums up how many viewers feel watching the movie. The 1959 film, directed by Ed Wood, told the story of an alien plot to take over the Earth by raising the dead.

The film is legendary for its incompetence. Police leave in one car and arrive in a different one. Inexplicably, scenes turn from day to night and back again. Actors knock over cardboard tombstones in a graveyard. Spaceships were made of paper plates dangled by strings. When the star of the film, Bela Lugosi, died after shooting only a few scenes, director Wood had the ingenious idea of having a chiropractor imitate Lugosi by holding a cape over the bottom half of his face. Unfortunately, the younger, taller man looked nothing like Lugosi. *Plan 9* is filled with inane dialogue, also written by Wood. When Inspector Clay, played by Tor Johnson, is killed, another policeman exclaims, "Inspector Clay's dead. Murdered. And one thing's for sure; somebody's responsible."

2. *MANOS, THE HANDS OF FATE*

Manos, The Hands of Fate was directed by Texas fertilizer salesman Harold Warren, who also starred in the film. The movie began with endless scenes of a family driving through a desolate landscape and went downhill from there. The plot concerned the Master, who enslaved a group of women dressed in negligees. His assistant, Torgo, has an unusual deformity: his thighs are twice the size of normal men's. As the creature hobbles around, the irritating Torgo theme is played.

The premise of the now defunct cult television series *Mystery Science Theater 3000* was to have mad scientist Clayton Forrester torture the crew of a spaceship by showing them bad movies. *Manos* was so bad Forrester actually apologized to his captive audience.

3. *THE CREEPING TERROR*

As its title suggests, *The Creeping Terror* is about a carpetlike monster from outer space that creeps around devouring the local populace. The monster actually was propelled by college students crawling beneath the carpet. When director Art Nelson lost the soundtrack to the movie, he cleverly hired an actor to explain what was happening. The narrator goes to ridiculous lengths to explain each character's motivation. One of the most absurd scenes is when the monster attacks a hootenanny. A young man heroically tries to beat off the monster with a guitar, to no avail. Director Nelson helped finance the film by having residents of Lake Tahoe, where the film was shot, pay for the privilege of acting in it, writing the music, and performing other tasks.

4. *MESA OF LOST WOMEN*

Mesa of Lost Women holds a special place in the heart of this author. I saw this film in the mid-1970s, before the Golden Turkey books, giving bad films their due, were published. The 1953 film stars Jackie Coogan, years before he played Uncle Fester on *The Addams Family,* as a mad scientist who creates a race of spider women. The film features a horrible flamenco guitar score that is certain to get on every viewer's nerves.

5. *RAT PFINK A BOO BOO*

Rat Pfink a Boo Boo was a lame attempt to parody the *Batman* television series. Rat Pfink reminds his fellow crimefighter, Boo Boo, that the only thing they have to fear is bullets. Much of the film is taken up with an endless low-speed chase on the crimefighters' Rat Cycle. At each intersection, Rat Pfink reminds Boo Boo to look both ways. Comic relief is provided by Kogar the Swinging Ape. The film reportedly cost $8,000 to make; one wonders where the money was spent.

6. *ROBOT MONSTER*

One of the most famous of all bad movies, *Robot Monster* features the most absurd monster in the history of cinema. Because the budget was so small, the filmmaker hired a man in a gorilla suit to play the space alien, Ro-Man, sent to conquer Earth with his deadly calcinator death ray. To make him even more ridiculous, he wore a diving helmet over his head. Ro-Man hides in a cave that emits bubbles, causing one to wonder if Lawrence Welk and his Champagne Music Makers are being held captive in it.

7. *GLEN OR GLENDA?*

Ed Wood strikes again in his most personal film. The cross-dressing director stars in the film about a man who wants nothing more than to wear his girlfriend's angora sweater. The film is padded shamelessly with stock footage of buffalo stampedes and other unrelated material. Bela Lugosi appears as the Puppet Master, whose incoherent narration speaks of "snakes and snails and puppy dog tails."

8. *THE BEAST OF YUCCA FLATS*

Tor Johnson gets a chance to expand his limited dramatic range by playing a Russian scientist. Unfortunately, he gets caught in a nuclear explosion that turns him into a monster. He spends the remainder of the movie walking through the desert, killing people, while the narrator tries to explain what is happening.

9. *MANIAC*

One of the most outrageous movies ever made was the 1934 film *Maniac*. Directed by Dwain Esper, the film tells the story of a deranged man who murders a mad doctor to steal his identity. One of the characters is a rapist who thinks he's a gorilla. The most disgusting moment occurs when main character pulls out a cat's eye and eats it.

10. *THE HORROR OF PARTY BEACH*

Of all the beach films of the 1960s, *The Horror of Party Beach* is undoubtedly the worst. Beach bunnies are terrorized by radioactive sea mutants who look as though they have hot dogs coming out of their mouths. The rock group the Bel-Aires provides catchy songs, such as *The Zombie Stomp.* At the end of the film, the seemingly indestructible monsters are destroyed when salt is thrown on them. The horror! The horror!

The Worst Directors of All Time

Not every director can be a Federico Fellini or Martin Scorsese. Some are doomed by low budgets, personal obsessions, or just a lack of talent. These directors are the auteurs of bad film.

1. **ED WOOD**

Actor Conrad Brooks said of director Ed Wood, "He wanted to make films in the worst way, and he did." Ed Wood created some of the worst films ever made: *Glen or Glenda?, Bride of the Monster, Plan 9 from Outer Space,* and *Night of the Ghouls* among them. The multitalented Wood directed, wrote, and sometimes starred in his films. His repertory company of actors included Bela Lugosi, Criswell, Tor Johnson, and Vampira. The prolific Wood also wrote dozens of adult novels, including *It Takes One to Know One, Death of a Transvestite, Bye Bye Broadie, The Perverts,* and *Purple Thighs.* His short stories include *The Balcony of Usher, That Damn Faceless Fog, Ever Hear a Dingbat,* and the classics, *Missionary Position Impossible* and *Captain Fellatio Hornblower.*

2. **RAY DENNIS STECKLER**

Like Ed Wood, Ray Dennis Steckler was a man of many talents. He was the cinematographer of films such as *The Erotic
Adventures of Pinocchio* and acted in his own films under the
alias Cash Flagg. Most important, he directed some of the
most bizarre films ever made. Steckler had a particular gift
for titles. Three of his most famous films are *The Incredibly
Strange Creatures Who Stopped Living and Became Mixed-Up
Zombies, Rat Pfink a Boo Boo,* and *The Lemon Grove Kids Meet
the Green Grasshopper and the Vampire Lady from Outer Space.*

3. **COLEMAN FRANCIS**

Like Ed Wood, Coleman Francis wrote, directed, and sometimes starred in his films. Francis is known to aficionados of
bad films for two turkeys, *The Beast of Yucca Flats* and *Red
Zone Cuba.* His films are characterized by incomprehensible
plots and endless scenes of fat men climbing on rocks.

4. **WILLIAM BEAUDINE**

William Beaudine directed 182 films during a career that lasted
from 1915 to 1966. He was known as "One Shot" Beaudine
because he rarely reshot a scene, even if it contained mis-
takes. His films have some of the worst titles of all time:
*Windbag the Sailor, Bela Lugosi Meets a Brooklyn Gorilla, Billy the
Kid vs. Dracula,* and *Jesse James Meets Frankenstein's Daughter.*

5. **PHIL TUCKER**

Phil Tucker is the director who brought the world *Robot
Monster,* the film about gorillas wearing diving helmets, who
take over the world. Reportedly, the young director was so
upset with the response to his film he attempted suicide.

According to *The Golden Turkey Awards,* the audience at his drag-strip drama, *Pachuco,* rioted at a Texas drive-in and destroyed the screen. His final film, *Cape Canaveral Monsters,* was about aliens who take over the bodies of decomposing corpses and attempt to disrupt the U.S. space program.

6. **TED MIKELS**

Another master of the bad film genre was Ted Mikels, cinematographer on such bad film classics as *Children Shouldn't Play with Dead Things* and *Catalina Caper.* Mikels produced the dreadful *The Undertaker and His Pals* and *The Worm Eaters,* but his reputation as a director rests on two films: *The Corpse Grinders* and *The Astro-Zombies.* In *The Corpse Grinders,* a pet food company makes cat food by grinding up human corpses. The plan backfires when the cats, liking the taste of human flesh, begin attacking their owners. Mikels spent $38 on the cardboard corpse-grinding machine. In *The Astro-Zombies,* mad scientist John Carradine creates a race of Astro-Zombies, who proceed to disembowel many of the townspeople.

7. **HERSCHELL GORDON LEWIS**

Herschell Gordon Lewis earned his reputation as the King of Gore with his films' scenes of incredible butchery. In *Blood Feast,* an Egyptian caterer murders women for their body parts. The most disgusting scene occurs when the caterer rips out a woman's tongue. Lewis achieved this not-so-special effect by having the actress conceal a sheep's tongue in her mouth. A character in *The Gore Gore Girls* pulls out a woman's eye and squeezes it until it pops. The artist in *Color Me Blood Red* murders his models to make red paint with their blood. Other Lewis gorefests are *2000 Maniacs* and *The Wizard of*

Gore, about Montag the Magician, who *really* saws women in half.

8. DORIS WISHMAN

Director Doris Wishman made a series of nudie films, but she is best known for her collaboration with actress Chesty Morgan. Ms. Morgan was famous for her amazing 73-inch chest. In *Double Agent 73,* Morgan plays a secret agent who has a camera implanted in her left breast. Chesty kills men in *Deadly Weapons* by smothering them with her humongous bosom.

9. DWAIN ESPER

Dwain Esper had been called the Father of the Exploitation Film. During the 1930s, he directed pictures that pushed the boundaries of what could be shown. His films have a delirious feel about them; some of his best known are *Maniac, Marihuana, Weed with Roots in Hell,* and *How to Undress in Front of Your Husband.*

10. ANDY MILLIGAN

Director Andy Milligan boasted that he never made a film that cost more than $10,000, and you know the old saying, "you get what you pay for." Some of Milligan's low-budget shockers include *The Degenerates, The Filthy Five, Gutter Trash, Bloodthirsty Butchers, Guru the Mad Monk, Fleshpot on 42nd Street,* and the incomparable *The Rats Are Coming! The Werewolves Are Here.*

In the Stars

B asil Rathbone, best known for his portrayal of Sherlock Holmes in the films about the famed detective, claimed to have ESP. Natalie Wood, who drowned in 1981, had a life-long fear of water. Director Erich von Stroheim frequently consulted fortune-tellers. Many Hollywood stars have had encounters with the unexplained.

1. CAROLE LOMBARD

On January 16, 1942, Carole Lombard was to return to Hollywood after participating in a war bond rally in Indianapolis. Her mother, Elizabeth, warned her that a numerologist had told her January 16 was a bad day for flying. Lombard was eager to return home and flipped a coin to decide whether they would fly or take the train. Lombard won the toss, and they decided to fly. It would be the first airplane flight for Lombard's mother—and her last. The plane crashed into Table Rock Mountain in Nevada, killing everyone aboard.

2. DAVID JANSSEN

David Janssen is best known for his role as Richard Kimble on the television series *The Fugitive.* On February 11, 1980,

Janssen had a disturbing dream that his coffin was being carried out of the house. Two days later, the 48-year-old actor died of a heart attack.

3. NANCY REAGAN

Nancy Reagan was at the center of a controversy when it was learned that she used astrology while her husband, Ronald, was President. She assured the public she used astrology as a way to cope with the assassination attempt on her husband. She said that it was used to determine the President's schedule, but was not consulted to help make policy decisions.

4. LUPE VELEZ

Actress Lupe Velez was warned by a fortune-teller she would die by her own hand, and Velez was haunted by the prediction. Years later, on December 14, 1944, the 36-year-old actress committed suicide at her home by taking a drug overdose.

5. PETER SELLERS

Comic actor Peter Sellers was told by a clairvoyant that he would marry a woman with the initials, B. E. The prediction came true when he married actress Britt Ekland on February 19, 1964, less than a month after they met.

6. RACHEL WARD

British beauty Rachel Ward claimed that tarot readings foretold many of the events in her life. Two of the most important predictions: she would become a movie star and would marry actor Bryan Brown. Both came true.

7. MIRIAM HOPKINS

Thirties star Miriam Hopkins liked to entertain guests at parties by reading palms and tarot cards. In addition, she depended on psychic advisors to help her select film projects and arrange her schedule. Hopkins would avoid certain locations if she was warned away from them by her numerologist.

8. MARY PICKFORD

Mary Pickford read her horoscope every day and made plans depending on whether or not the reading was favorable. It must have worked, because Pickford was one of the most popular and wealthiest stars of her time.

9. BOB CUMMINGS

Bob Cummings, who starred in *Kings Row* and *Saboteur*, believed strongly in astrology. Reportedly, Cummings never left home without consulting his astrology chart.

10. SESSUE HAYAKAWA

Silent film actor Sessue Hayakawa claimed to have psychic powers, the most remarkable of which was his ability to read unopened letters.

Haunted Hollywood

Actress Robin Givens claimed her house was haunted by the ghost of a former owner, Beatle John Lennon. Occidental Studios reportedly was haunted by stagehands who had fallen to their deaths while filming movies there. It is said as well that many departed stars still walk the streets and roam the back lots of Hollywood.

1. MAE WEST

Mae West always believed she had a special affinity with the spirit world, and she frequently consulted psychics and fortune-tellers. West died in November 1980, but her ghost is said to still occupy her home in the Ravenswood Apartments, where she lived for 50 years. Her reflection has been seen in mirrors, and her presence is felt often by residents who sometimes leave drinks out for her.

2. RUDOLPH VALENTINO

Rudolph Valentino died in 1926 at the age of 31. His ex-wife, Natasha Rambova, claimed Valentino spoke to her from the afterworld through a medium. She said Valentino told her he had been reunited with other deceased stars, Wallace Reid, Olive Thomas, and Barbara La Marr. Valentino's home, Falcon Lair, also was said to be haunted by his ghost. Guests reported hearing footsteps and seeing doors open and close, and one woman even claimed the ghost of Valentino kissed her while she was lying on the bed.

3. SHARON TATE

One of the most disturbing ghost stories happened to actress Sharon Tate in 1966. Tate was staying overnight at the home of Jay Sebring, who was away. While in bed, she saw the figure of a creepy little man who kept bumping into things. Terrified by the apparition, she ran downstairs, only to encounter a much more frightening sight. At the foot of the stairs, she saw a figure tied to the banister with her throat cut. The house had belonged to Jean Harlow, and it was there Harlow's husband, Paul Bern, had committed suicide by shooting himself. The ghost of the small man in the bedroom reportedly resembled Bern. The grisly apparition at the bottom of the stairs was a premonition of her own death, however; Tate was slashed to death by followers of Charles Manson at her home on August 9, 1969.

4. CLIFTON WEBB

Clifton Webb was a brilliant character actor, best known for his performance in *Laura*. After Webb died in 1966, his house was sold to columnist Joyce Haber, who experienced a number of unnerving incidents, such as doors opening and closing. The strangest thing was that she kept finding her cigarettes ripped to shreds. One day she saw the ghost of Clifton Webb, who abhorred smoking, tearing up a pack of her cigarettes in the bathroom.

5. JAYNE MANSFIELD

Jayne Mansfield loved living in her home, which she called the Pink Palace. She loved it so much she never left, not even after her death in an automobile accident in 1967. Singer Engelbert Humperdinck, who bought the home years later, said he saw the ghost of Mansfield, in a revealing dress, walking down the staircase.

6. SAM KINISON

The famous Hollywood nightclub Ciro's was the favorite of movie stars during the 1930s. Ciro's was also the hangout of gangsters, and it was rumored that a mobster had been murdered in the basement. Ciro's eventually closed, and many years later, it became The Comedy Store, the club that launched the careers of many of today's top comics. The ghosts of gangsters who reportedly still haunt The Comedy Store apparently didn't like comedian Sam Kinison. The spirits frequently tried to disrupt his performance by making the lights flicker and committing other mischief. Kinison even issued challenges to the ghosts. Andrew Dice Clay recalled that he and Kinison once walked upstairs to where a door was padlocked. When a banging sound was heard suddenly from behind the locked door, Kinison and Clay ran down the stairs, not wishing to find out what was behind the door.

7. LAURENCE HARVEY

Acclaimed British actor Laurence Harvey died in 1973. Comedian Flip Wilson, who bought Harvey's Malibu Beach home in the 1970s, said he frequently saw Harvey's ghost in the home, particularly standing near the bar. Wilson had the house cleansed by a paranormal expert, and Harvey's ghost was never seen again.

8. **MONTGOMERY CLIFT**

Montgomery Clift stayed in Room 928 of the Roosevelt Hotel in Hollywood for three months in 1953 during the filming of *From Here to Eternity*. He played a bugler in the film and practiced playing the instrument in his room. Clift died in 1966. Guests staying in Room 928 have reported hearing Clift still practicing playing the bugle. They've also reported hearing voices and seeing furniture move by itself.

9. **MARILYN MONROE**

Another uninvited guest of the Roosevelt Hotel is Marilyn Monroe. A maid said she saw Monroe's reflection in the mirror of a room where the blonde actress had stayed once. Since Monroe's death in 1962, her ghost reportedly has been spotted in Hollywood many times.

10. **THOMAS INCE**

Director Thomas Ince died in November 1924. In 1988, the studio where Ince made many of his films was being demolished. According to two of the workers, the ghost of Ince walked up to them and said, "I don't like what you're doing."

Hollywood's Urban Legends

An urban legend is a fantastic rumor that may or may not be true—no one's ever sure. Over the years, many urban legends have originated in Hollywood.

1. JOHN GILBERT

John Gilbert, one of the most popular leading men of the silent film era, had frequent run-ins with MGM studio head Louis B. Mayer. After one altercation, Mayer supposedly said that he would ruin Gilbert, even if it cost him a million dollars. At the screening of Gilbert's first talking film, *His Glorious Night,* audiences laughed at his acting and his high voice. Gilbert's talkie was referred to as a "shriekie." Rumor was Mayer had the sound technicians tamper with Gilbert's voice to destroy his career. True or not, Gilbert's career took a nosedive when talkies replaced silent films.

2. CLARA BOW

Clara Bow was the biggest Hollywood sex symbol of the 1920s. She was linked romantically with many male stars, and it was rumored that she was promiscuous. A joke circulated around Hollywood that Clara "laid everything except the linoleum." In 1927, she became a fan of the University of Southern California football team, known as the Thundering Herd. An avid supporter of the team, she invited them to her Bedford Drive mansion to celebrate their victories. Reportedly, Bow was having a romance with the team captain, Morley Drury. There was talk that nude football games were being played on Bow's lawn, and some believed that Bow had actually gang-banged the entire Trojan team. Only the players knew for sure, but the USC coach soon declared Clara Bow off-limits to his players.

3. LUPE VELEZ

Lupe Velez committed suicide by taking an overdose of sleeping pills on December 14, 1944. The accepted account was that she was found the next morning, lying peacefully on her bed. A less dignified story has become an urban legend, however. Velez had wanted to die a death befitting a Hollywood star, so she filled her bedroom with fragrant tuberoses and gardenias and illuminated the room with candlelight. Then she put on her best blue satin pajamas and swallowed 75 Seconal tablets. She expected to be discovered the next morning, looking beautiful. Unfortunately, her last meal had been a Mexican feast, and the combination of the spicy food and the pills caused her to be nauseated. Half-conscious, she staggered to the bathroom, leaving a trail of vomit. She slipped on the tiles and fell headfirst in the toilet.

4. JAYNE MANSFIELD

Was Jayne Mansfield involved in satanism? In November 1966, Mansfield visited Anton LaVey, the high priest of the Church of Satan. When Mansfield's five-year-old son, Zoltan, was mauled by a lion at Jungleland, it was said that she went to LaVey to make a deal to save his life. Zoltan recovered, but Jayne Mansfield was killed in an automobile accident on June 29, 1967. Had she somehow been cursed by the satanic association? Reportedly, LaVey had accidentally cut off Mansfield's head in a photograph . . . and Jayne was nearly decapitated in the accident.

5. JOHN BARRYMORE

John Barrymore died on May 29, 1942. According to director Raoul Walsh, he and a few of Barrymore's drinking buddies removed the corpse from the Malloy Brothers Mortuary and took it to Errol Flynn's house. They propped Barrymore on the couch and waited for Flynn to return. Flynn took one look at the body and ran.

6. JAMES DEAN

James Dean was driving his new silver Porsche Spyder convertible when he was killed in an automobile accident on September 30, 1955. The car, which Dean referred to as the Little Bastard, reportedly was cursed. Custom car designer George Barris purchased the wrecked Porsche, but when it was delivered, it inexplicably came loose from the truck transporting it and broke a mechanic's legs. The engine of the death car was sold to a doctor named Troy McHenry, who put it into another Porsche and was killed in an accident the first time he drove it. Barris sold the transmission to another man, who was paralyzed in an accident while driving the car. Finally, the shell of the Porsche was loaded onto a truck to be put on display in a traveling exhibit; the truck subsequently crashed, and the shell disappeared.

Floyd Conner

Notorious party animal John Barrymore was dead when he reportedly had a role in a practical joke on Errol Flynn.

7. **THOMAS INCE**

Director Thomas Ince was one of the guests invited to cruise on William Randolph Hearst's yacht, *The Oneida,* in November 1924. Other guests included Hearst's mistress, Marion Davies; Charlie Chaplin; and columnist Louella Parsons, who had just arrived in Hollywood. On November 19, the 42-year-old Ince died suddenly. Although the official story was that Ince died of a stomach disorder, a rumor spread that Hearst accidentally shot Ince. Hearst suspected that Davies was having an affair with Chaplin. He supposedly caught the two together, but somehow shot Ince by mistake. Reportedly, Louella Parsons was given a lifetime contract with the Hearst newspapers for not revealing the truth about Ince's death.

8. **LUCILLE BALL**

The Communist scare of the early 1950s ruined the careers of many actors and even threatened America's favorite redhead, Lucille Ball. When it was disclosed that Ball had registered as a Communist when she voted in 1936, she said she had done so as a favor to her grandfather, who had leftist leanings. Ball was asked to testify before the House Un-American Activities Committee on September 4, 1953, where it was suggested that Ball not only was a registered Communist, but that she had been a delegate to the Central Party Committee. Ball admitted she had registered as a Communist, but denied any other involvement. Her husband, Desi Arnaz, said that the only thing red about Lucy was her hair. Ball survived the controversy, and America continued to love Lucy.

9. *THE WIZARD OF OZ*

A grisly rumor has circulated for years concerning a possible suicide on the set of *The Wizard of Oz*. The story goes that a despondent crew member hung himself during filming. Many viewers of the film contend that his body can be seen swinging in the background of the Enchanted Forest. Those involved in the film totally denied the claim; they explained the movement as the flight of a bird.

10. *THREE MEN AND A BABY*

There's a scene in the 1987 hit film *Three Men and a Baby* where Olympia Dukakis lifts a baby out of a crib. In the background, it appears as if a child's face is looking through the window. People began speculating the child was a ghost, but Touchstone Pictures explained it was just a promotional cut-out of star Ted Danson that had been left there by mistake.

The Unkindest Cut

The film censor's job is to delete anything deemed offensive in a movie. In many instances, censorship has bordered on the ridiculous, however. In the 1932 film *Madame Butterfly*, a scene was cut because it showed Sylvia Sidney's bare elbow.

1. *THE HYPOCRITES*

The Hypocrites, a 1915 film directed by Lois Weber, featured a brief scene of a nude woman who symbolized the naked truth. The mayor of Boston insisted that clothes be painted on the print frame by frame before he would permit the film to be shown in his city.

2. TOKYO PREFECT OF POLICE

In 1926, the Tokyo Prefect of Police declared that kissing was immodest and likely to spread disease. He censored more than 800,000 feet of kissing scenes from American films.

3. *THE MUPPET MOVIE*

The Muppet Movie was a favorite family film everywhere when it was released in 1979, except in New Zealand. In that country, a scene involving Fozzie Bear was cut for what the censor deemed was gratuitous violence. The banned scene involved Fozzie in a confrontation with a drunken sailor.

4. **MICKEY MOUSE**

Mickey Mouse, one of the most beloved cartoon characters of all time, was banned in Romania in 1935 because censors felt he was frightening to children. Incredibly, Mickey was banned for a time in Italy, Germany, and Russia as well.

5. *SNOW WHITE AND THE SEVEN DWARFS*

Another Disney classic, *Snow White and the Seven Dwarfs,* had censorship problems. A scene in which the dwarfs were making up Snow White's bed was cut because audiences might think the dwarfs were having sex with her.

6. *TREASURE ISLAND*

Censors frequently try to ban films they believe contribute to the delinquency of minors. Censors in Ohio tried to ban the 1920 film version of the Robert Louis Stevenson classic *Treasure Island,* because it might encourage children to become pirates.

7. **JOHN DILLINGER**

John Dillinger was shot to death outside the Biograph Theater in July 1934. Although the last hours of his life were spent watching a crime drama, *Manhattan Melodrama,* it would be years before Dillinger's life was depicted on screen. It was illegal to make a film in the United States about Dillinger for 10 years after his death because government officials were concerned his life might be glorified.

8. *GOING MY WAY*

Bing Crosby won an Academy Award for his portrayal of a priest in *Going My Way*. The film was banned in several countries in Latin America because the priest wore a sweatshirt and ball cap in one scene, instead of his religious garb.

9. *FROM THIS DAY FORWARD*

From This Day Forward, a 1946 film starring Joan Fontaine, included the lines, "I didn't sleep well last night. It must have been the two cups of coffee I drank last night." The last line was omitted because it might offend Brazilian coffee growers.

10. *THE SPIRIT OF '76*

The Spirit of '76 was a 1917 film about the Revolutionary War. It was banned in Chicago because of its negative depiction of the British, who were America's allies during World War I.

Fighting Mad

*R*aging Bull, Champion, Somebody Up There Likes Me, and *The Set Up* are classic Hollywood boxing movies. Sometimes stars, directors, and even movie moguls fought off-screen as well. Sean Penn is one of many stars who have had run-ins with photographers invading their privacy. In 1983, Ryan O'Neal knocked out his son Griffin's front teeth during a fight.

1. LOUIS B. MAYER VS. SAM GOLDWYN

MGM studio head Louis B. Mayer got into a fight with his fellow movie mogul, Sam Goldwyn, in the showers of the Hillcrest Country Club. Mayer knocked Goldwyn into the towel cabinet, and Goldwyn threatened to sue Mayer for a million dollars. Goldwyn wasn't the first person to feel the power of Mayer's punch. The latter decked Erich von Stroheim during filming of *The Merry Widow* after von Stroheim commented, "all women are whores." Mayer also sucker punched Charlie Chaplin during an argument over remarks Chaplin made about his ex-wife, Mildred.

2. **AVA GARDNER VS. HOWARD HUGHES**

During an argument, Howard Hughes slapped Ava Gardner so hard he dislocated her jaw. Gardner responded by breaking a vase over the millionaire's head. Hughes was knocked cold and suffered two broken teeth.

3. **ERROL FLYNN VS. JOHN HUSTON**

Director John Huston sometimes got into fights when he had too much to drink. He met his match when he challenged Errol Flynn at a party. Flynn floored Huston with a combination. When Flynn tried to help him to his feet, Huston insisted on continuing the fight. Flynn knocked Huston out cold and then poured water on him to revive him. He warned the director that he had been a professional prizefighter and Huston could never beat him. Huston didn't take his advice and was knocked out again.

4. **TOM NEAL VS. FRANCHOT TONE**

Actors Tom Neal and Franchot Tone were rivals for the affection of actress Barbara Payton. On September 14, 1951, the two men fought in front of Payton's Hollywood Hills home. Neal, a former amateur boxer, gave Tone a merciless beating. Tone was hospitalized with a fractured cheek and broken nose, and Payton suffered a black eye when she was hit by an errant punch. Two weeks later, Payton and Tone, still showing the effects of the beating, were married. In May 1952, Payton divorced Tone and returned to Neal.

5. **OLEG CASSINI VS. HOWARD HUGHES**

There was no love lost between Oleg Cassini and Howard Hughes. Cassini did not appreciate Hughes's romantic interest in his wife, Gene Tierney. Once, when he caught Hughes bringing Tierney home, he leaped out of the shadows and punched him in the face. Cassini then chased Hughes down Wilshire Boulevard before the producer reached the safety of his penthouse. On another occasion, Hughes locked himself in the bedroom after seeing Cassini at a party.

6. LUPE VELEZ VS. LILYAN TASHMAN

Actresses Lupe Velez and Lilyan Tashman both knew how to throw a punch. The fiery Velez could more than hold her own in battles with men, and Tashman had faced charges for beating Alona Marlowe when Tashman caught her in husband Edmund Lowe's dressing room. The catfight between Velez and Tashman took place in the powder room of the Montmartre Café in Hollywood; the two women clawed and punched each other on the floor of the powder room. By all accounts, Velez won a clear decision.

7. FANNY BRICE VS. LILLIAN LORRAINE

Fanny Brice's life was depicted in the film *Funny Girl,* a role that won Barbra Streisand an Oscar. Brice once got into a backstage fight with famed stage actress Lillian Lorraine. Lorraine was angry about Brice's involvement with her husband, Fred Gersheimer. Lorraine was apparently no match for Brice, however; after knocking Lorraine down, Brice dragged her by the hair onto the stage to the approval of the crowd.

8. TOMMY SANDS VS. KEVIN THOMAS

Singer-actor Tommy Sands took exception to a review by critic Kevin Thomas in the *Los Angeles Times.* Thomas called Sands's performance in the 1965 film *None but the Brave* "hammy." Sands went to Thomas's office at the *Times* and punched him. What perplexed Thomas was that the review had been published nine months before the assault. Thomas mused, "He must have been a slow reader."

9. **WILLIAM WELLMAN VS. SPENCER TRACY**

William Wellman, director of such classics as *The Ox Bow Incident, The Public Enemy,* and *Nothing Sacred,* got into a fight with Spencer Tracy on December 4, 1935, at the Café Trocadero, a popular Hollywood nightspot. Wellman had made disparaging remarks about Loretta Young, with whom Tracy was romantically involved at the time. Wellman, who had the reputation of being a tough guy, decked Tracy, who'd had one drink too many.

10. **GRETA GARBO VS. GEORGE BRENT**

Greta Garbo hardly seemed like the fighting kind, but she occasionally donned boxing gloves. She and actor George Brent liked to spar in his backyard.

Feuds for Thought

When big stars work together, egos occasionally clash. John Barrymore and Katherine Hepburn, who co-starred in the 1932 film *A Bill of Divorcement,* clashed on the set. Wallace Beery and Jean Harlow, the stars of *Dinner at Eight,* loathed one another. Mercedes McCambridge was one of the many actresses who disliked Joan Crawford.

1. BETTE DAVIS AND JOAN CRAWFORD

The most intense feud in Hollywood history was between two of its biggest female stars, Bette Davis and Joan Crawford. The feud began in 1935 when Davis's leading man in *Dangerous* was Crawford's husband, Franchot Tone. When Davis and Tone became romantically involved, Crawford understandably was outraged. Davis was quick to point out Crawford's reputation with men: "She's slept with every male star at MGM except Lassie."

In 1962, the aging stars were cast as sisters who were former child stars in *Whatever Happened to Baby Jane?* In the film, a resentful Davis, playing Baby Jane, does horrible things to her invalid sister, played by Crawford, including serving her a rat for dinner. Davis relished the role and recalled, "The best time I ever had with Joan Crawford was the time I pushed her down the stairs in *Whatever Happened to Baby Jane?*" Davis was nominated for an Oscar for Best Actress for her performance as Baby Jane. Crawford got the last laugh, however, when she gleefully accepted the Oscar for an absent Anne Bancroft for her performance in *The Miracle Worker.* The feud lasted right to the very end.

When Davis learned of Crawford's death in 1977, she said, "Well, the bitch is dead." In 1985, Davis donated 59 scrapbooks to Boston University. All of the photos of Joan Crawford had her teeth blacked out.

2. OLIVIA DE HAVILLAND AND JOAN FONTAINE

The feud between sisters Olivia de Havilland and Joan Fontaine began in childhood. Fontaine remembered that they pulled each other's hair and wrestled. It was so rough de Havilland actually broke her sister's collarbone. Fontaine won the Academy Award for Best Actress for her performance in the 1941 film *Suspicion.* Even then she expressed fear her sister would leap across the table and grab her hair. Five years later, Olivia de Havilland won her first Oscar for her performance in *To Each His Own.* Fontaine reached out to shake her hand, but de Havilland walked right by her.

3. WALTER MATTHAU AND BARBRA STREISAND

Walter Matthau co-starred with Barbra Streisand in the 1969 film *Hello, Dolly!* Veteran actor Matthau did not take it kindly when Streisand began offering acting suggestions. Matthau barked, "You may be the singer in this picture, but I'm the actor." Matthau boasted he had more talent in his fart than she had in her whole body. She referred to him as "Old

Sewer Mouth," and he called her "Miss Ptomaine." When Matthau discovered he was the number 10 box office attraction, one spot below Streisand, he commented, "Can you imagine being under Barbra Streisand? Get me a bag. I may throw up."

4. **BETTE DAVIS AND MIRIAM HOPKINS**

If any actress could give Bette Davis, the most difficult actress in Hollywood, a run for her money, it was Miriam Hopkins. Davis said of Hopkins, "I don't think there was ever a more difficult female in the world." The feud began early in their careers when they were in the same stock company in New York. Hopkins was the star, and she made sure the younger actress was fired. In 1943, Davis and Hopkins co-starred in *Old Acquaintances* and fought on and off the screen.

5. **BETTE DAVIS AND ERROL FLYNN**

Bette Davis disliked Errol Flynn almost as much as she detested Joan Crawford. They were co-starring in the 1939 film *The Private Lives of Elizabeth and Essex,* when the actress slapped Flynn so hard in one scene she almost knocked him out. Davis removed herself from consideration for the role of Scarlett O'Hara in *Gone With the Wind* because she thought Flynn would be cast as Rhett Butler. The only thing about which she ever agreed with Flynn was his admission that he knew nothing about acting.

6. **FRANK SINATRA AND MARLON BRANDO**

Frank Sinatra and Marlon Brando did not get along during the filming of *Guys and Dolls* in 1955. Sinatra preferred to do one take, while Brando preferred multiple takes. In one scene, Sinatra was forced to eat several pieces of cheesecake when Brando insisted on take after take. "How much fucking cheesecake can a man eat?" Frank fumed. Sinatra referred to Brando as "Mumbles."

7. **MARLON BRANDO AND ROD STEIGER**

Marlon Brando gave his most acclaimed performance as an ex-boxer in the 1954 film *On the Waterfront*. Rod Steiger played his older brother. The most famous scene in the movie featured Brando and Steiger in the backseat of a car. Brando gave his "I coulda been a contender" speech to his brother, who had encouraged him to take a dive in his big fight. In one rehearsal, Brando left the set, forcing Steiger to read his lines on empty set. Steiger didn't speak to Brando for 43 years.

8. **ORSON WELLES AND PETER SELLERS**

Orson Welles and Peter Sellers appeared in the James Bond spoof *Casino Royale*. Welles disliked Sellers so much Welles refused to do a scene with him. He insisted they shoot their scenes on separate days, so each had to speak his lines to a dummy.

9. **KLAUS KINSKI AND WERNER HERZOG**

Director Werner Herzog and actor Klaus Kinski had a turbulent relationship. Herzog pulled a gun on Kinski when the actor threatened to walk out on the 1972 film *Aguirre, Wrath of God*. Ten years later, during the filming of *Fitzcarraldo*, Herzog reportedly tried to burn down the house Kinski was sleeping in. Herzog said about Kinski, "The best thing to happen to his career is for him to die immediately."

10. **JOAN CRAWFORD AND MARILYN MONROE**

By the time Marilyn Monroe was a young star in the early 1950s, Joan Crawford was an aging star who represented the Hollywood establishment. Crawford was appalled at Monroe's blatant sexuality: "She has no girdle on and her ass was hanging out. She's a disgrace to the motion picture industry."

Scandalous Behavior

Since the beginning of film, movie stars have been involved in scandals. From Fatty Arbuckle to Eddie Murphy, the private lives of stars have been fodder for the tabloids. The scandals have involved sexual indiscretions, drug busts, even murder. Relive some of the biggest scandals in Hollywood history. Some of the stars' careers survived them, others' did not.

1. FATTY ARBUCKLE

Fatty Arbuckle was one of the biggest (both in popularity and size) stars of his day. On September 5, 1921, Arbuckle threw a Labor Day party at the St. Francis Hotel in San Francisco. Arbuckle and starlet Virginia Rappe retired to a bedroom. Later, guests found Rappe lying nude on the floor, moaning, "Roscoe hurt me, I'm dying." Rappe was taken to the hospital, where she died three days later. There was speculation that Arbuckle had crushed the petite Rappe with his 300-pound weight during sex. An even uglier accusation claimed he had violated her with a soda pop bottle. Arbuckle endured three trials before he was finally acquitted, but the public never forgave him. Although he did direct a few film shorts under the alias Will B. Goode, Arbuckle died a broken man in 1933 at age 46.

2. LANA TURNER

In 1958, Lana Turner faced a real-life drama more serious than any she confronted in the many tearjerkers she starred in. Her lover, Johnny Stompanato, former bodyguard of mobster Mickey Cohen, was stabbed to death in Turner's Bedford Drive home. Turner said her 14-year-old daughter, Cheryl Crane, had stabbed Stompanato in the stomach with a nine-inch kitchen knife when he threatened Turner. At the inquest to investigate the stabbing, Stompanato's death was ruled a justifiable homicide. Turner's tearful appearance on the witness stand was considered to be one of her best performances. Although some unsavory aspects of Turner's love life were exposed, she emerged a bigger star than ever.

3. INGRID BERGMAN

Ingrid Bergman was at the height of her popularity in 1949, when she went to Italy to film *Stromboli* for director Roberto Rossellini. Although still married to Dr. Peter Lindstrom, she began an affair with Rossellini and had his child. The ensuing scandal jeopardized her career. Bergman made a comeback in 1956, when she won an Academy Award for her performance in *Anastasia.*

4. CLARA BOW

In 1931, Clara Bow accused her private secretary, Daisy DeVoe, of embezzling $16,000 of her money. DeVoe was convicted and sentenced to a year in jail, but Bow proved to be the real loser. DeVoe sold stories to the tabloids, revealing Bow's promiscuous love life. The ensuing bad publicity finished Bow's already waning acting career.

5. **MARY ASTOR**

Actress Mary Astor was married to Dr. Franklyn Thorpe in 1935 when she began a passionate affair with playwright George S. Kaufman. Thorpe learned of the affair when he found Astor's diary, which described her sex life with Kaufman in great detail. Astor swooned over Kaufman's prowess as a lover and his incredible staying power. The diary became public during the Thorpe/Astor divorce trial, but Astor's career was not harmed. She won an Oscar for Best Supporting Actress in 1941 for her performance in *The Great Lie,* and appeared in the classic films *The Maltese Falcon, The Palm Beach Story*, and *Meet Me in St. Louis.*

6. **ELIZABETH TAYLOR**

Elizabeth Taylor had more than her share of scandals. The biggest took place after the death of her third husband, Mike Todd, in a plane crash. Taylor began an affair with Todd's best friend, singer Eddie Fisher, who was married to Debbie Reynolds. The public sympathized with Reynolds, and Taylor was depicted as a homewrecker. In 1963, Taylor made headlines again when she dumped husband Eddie Fisher for her *Cleopatra* costar, Richard Burton.

7. **ERROL FLYNN**

Errol Flynn's preference for teenage girls nearly landed him in jail. In 1942, two underage girls, Peggy Satterlee and Betty Hansen, charged that Flynn seduced them. Flynn was tried for statutory rape, but, after a highly publicized trial, he was acquitted. The trial only seemed to enhance Flynn's legendary reputation as a lover.

8. **ROMAN POLANSKI**

Director Roman Polanski has made many critically acclaimed films, such as *Chinatown* and *Knife in the Water.* In 1977, he shot a photo session with a 13-year-old model in Jack Nicholson's home. Ordered to face trial on charges he'd had sex with the underage girl, Polanski fled to Paris and has yet to return to America. Polanski's next film, *Tess,* was a critical and box office success in the United States.

9. **PAUL REUBENS**

On July 28, 1991, comedian Paul Reubens was arrested at the South Trail Cinema in Sarasota, Florida, for allegedly masturbating while watching an adult film. Reubens gained fame as Pee Wee Herman, a childlike character in an ill-fitting gray suit. He had starred in the Tim Burton film *Pee Wee's Big Adventure,* and hosted the popular children's series *Pee Wee's Playhouse.* The scandal derailed his career as Pee Wee Herman, but he made a strong comeback as Paul Reubens, with appearances in films such as *Blow* and a role on the television sitcom *Murphy Brown.* In November 2001, Los Angeles police raided the comedian's home and seized his large collection of erotica.

10. **HUGH GRANT**

In June 1995, English actor Hugh Grant was caught being administered oral sex by a prostitute named Divine Brown in Los Angeles. The incident not only threatened Grant's acting career, but his relationship with actress, Elizabeth Hurley, as well. Hurley refused to discuss the matter in public, saying, "Brits think it's very unpleasant to open up a can of worms. You don't know what you might discover." Grant's career was not affected, but he and Hurley eventually broke up.

Go Directly to Jail

S ean Penn, Robert Downey Jr., Mark Wahlberg, Jan-Michael Vincent, Christian Slater, Kelsey Grammer, and Ryan O'Neal are just a few of the stars who have served time in jail.

1. ROBERT MITCHUM

Robert Mitchum was arrested for marijuana possession in August 1948, a time when a drug charge could destroy a career. When asked his occupation by the police, Mitchum replied, "Former actor." Mitchum served two months in jail, which he called the "best damn vacation" he'd had in years. Mitchum's antihero persona was not harmed by the jail time, and he went on to star in such films as *Night of the Hunter* and *Cape Fear.*

2. WALTER WANGER

Producer Walter Wanger was married to actress Joan Bennett. He suspected that his wife was having an affair with agent Jennings Lang, and Wanger vowed he "was going to take care of the man attempting to break up my marriage."

On December 13, 1951, Wanger shot Lang in the groin.
Wanger served three months in jail, and Lang lost a testicle.

3. RORY CALHOUN

Before he became a movie star, Rory Calhoun served three
years in Springfield State Prison for car theft. The public became aware of the old conviction when it made headlines in
Confidential magazine in the late 1950s. Calhoun's career
survived the revelations.

4. TIM ALLEN

Tim Allen served 28 months in jail after selling $43,000 of
cocaine to an undercover agent. Allen later starred in the
long-running sitcom *Home Improvement,* and films such as
The Santa Clause and *Toy Story.* Allen has spoken openly
about the incident, which has not affected his popularity.

5. SOPHIA LOREN

Sophia Loren spent 17 days in jail in her native Italy in 1982
after a conviction for income tax evasion. The incident didn't
damage Loren's reputation as an international superstar.

6. MAE WEST

Mae West served 10 days in jail on Welfare Island in New
York when her play *Sex* was declared obscene. West's sen-
tence was reduced by two days for good behavior.

7. MARK FRECHETTE

Mark Frechette starred in Michelangelo Antonioni's 1970
film *Zabriskie Point.* Three years later, Frechette was arrested
for a bank robbery in Boston. He died in prison in 1975 at

the age of 27 in a freak accident: he was lifting weights when a 160-pound weight fell on his throat.

8. **ZSA ZSA GABOR**

In 1989, Zsa Zsa Gabor served three days in jail after slapping a policeman during a traffic stop: she claimed the officer had dragged her out of her car. Gabor, no stranger to outrageous behavior, later made light of the incident.

9. **RUDOLPH VALENTINO**

Before he became a star, Rudolph Valentino served three days in jail in 1916. The charge was suspicion of being a gigolo.

10. **STACY KEACH**

Stacy Keach appeared in such films as *The Heart Is a Lonely Hunter* and *Brewster McCloud.* He also starred on television as private eye Mike Hammer. On April 4, 1984, Keach was busted for cocaine possession at Heathrow Airport in London. He served nine months in Reading Gaol.

Ending It All

Hollywood is a place of dreams, but sometimes the dreams don't come true. Dozens of actors have taken their own lives.

1. PEG ENTWISTLE

Peg Entwistle was an attractive blonde English actress who came to Hollywood in 1932. She had a small role in *Thirteen Women*, a film starring Myrna Loy and Irene Dunne, but the picture was shelved after a disappointing screening. To make matters worse, her studio option was dropped as well. Despondent, Entwistle climbed to the top of the HOLLYWOODLAND sign (which has since been shortened to read, "HOLLY-WOOD"), and jumped 50 feet to her death. Her suicide note read: "If I had done this a long time ago, I would have saved myself a lot of pain." Entwistle was 24 years old at the time of her death.

2. CLARA BLANDICK

Clara Blandick's acting career spanned four decades, but she will be remembered always for her role as Aunty Em in *The*

Wizard of Oz. In 1962, the 81-year-old actress, in failing health and losing her sight, decided to commit suicide in her Hollywood apartment. She put on her prettiest dress and placed memorabilia from her film career around her. Blandick swallowed a handful of sleeping pills and, to make sure the job was done right, tied a plastic bag around her head.

3. **LOU TELLEGEN**

Lou Tellegen was a silent film actor who starred in such films as *No Man Put Asunder* and *The Long Trail.* By 1935, his film career was over. Tellegen surrounded himself with scrapbooks, photos, and posters of his acting career, then grabbed a pair of scissors and jabbed them into his chest and stomach repeatedly until he bled to death.

4. **JOHN BOWERS**

Another silent film star who didn't make a successful transition to talking pictures was John Bowers. In the 1920s, Bowers starred in many films, including *Lorna Doone* and *Richard the Lion-Hearted.* On November 17, 1936, he rented a sailboat in Malibu and sailed off into the sunset. His body later washed ashore at Huntington Beach. Bowers was the inspiration for the suicide of character Norman Maine in *A Star Is Born.*

5. **FLORENCE LAWRENCE**

Florence Lawrence was the original Biograph (studios) Girl and the first actress to become a recognized star. For a time her popularity rivaled that of Mary Pickford. In 1914, Lawrence was seriously injured when she fell down a staircase filming *Pawns of Destiny.* She suffered a debilitating back injury, and her beautiful face was scarred. She made numerous comeback attempts, but her film career essentially was finished. In

1938, two days after Christmas, the 52-year-old former star ingested ant paste and died an agonizing death.

6. KARL DANE

Karl Dane was a Danish actor who received rave reviews for his performance of a doomed soldier in the 1925 film *The Big Parade.* Dane's heavy accent kept him from getting work in talking pictures, and he was reduced to opening a hot dog stand near a studio gate. On April 14, 1934, Dane spread out on the table old clippings, contracts, and reviews from his glory days, picked up a revolver, and shot himself in the head.

7. IRENE GIBBONS

Irene Gibbons was one of Hollywood's best costume design-ers. At MGM she designed gowns for Elizabeth Taylor, Judy Garland, Lana Turner, and many other glamorous actresses. In 1962, Irene became depressed and no longer seemed to be interested in living. On November 15, she checked into a room at Los Angeles's Knickerbocker Hotel. Irene slashed her wrists and jumped out the 14th-story window. She land-ed on an awning, and her body was not discovered until days later.

8. PIER ANGELI

Pier Angeli was an up-and-coming actress in the 1950s, who starred opposite Paul Newman in *Somebody Up There Likes Me.* Angeli was James Dean's girlfriend and wanted to marry him. Her mother disapproved of Dean, and Pier was pushed into marrying singer Vic Damone. Angeli was devastated when Dean was killed in an automobile accident; her career went downhill, and her marriage collapsed. After Dean's death she said, "Love is behind me; love died in a Porsche." On September 11, 1971, the 38-year-old actress committed suicide by overdosing on barbiturates.

9. JEAN SEBERG

Jean Seberg was an Iowa college student when she was discovered by director Otto Preminger in 1957 and signed to play Joan of Arc in his film *Saint Joan*. The beautiful Seberg starred in a series of films, including *Breathless, The Mouse That Roared,* and *Lilith.* Her radical political views were a contributing factor to her demise. The FBI kept her under surveillance because she was known to be a supporter of the Black Panther party. When she became pregnant, it was rumored the father was one of the Black Panthers. Although she miscarried the baby, Seberg displayed the infant's body in a glass coffin to prove it was white. She became increasingly paranoid and attempted suicide almost every year on the anniversary of the miscarriage. She finally succeeded on her seventh attempt in 1979. Her body was discovered in her automobile, days after the 40-year-old had taken an overdose of barbiturates. Seberg once said, "Money does buy happiness. But happiness isn't everything."

10. MARGARET SULLAVAN

Margaret Sullavan was one of the most enchanting actresses in film history. She gave wonderful performances in films such as *The Good Fairy* and *The Shop Around the Corner.* Depressed over the loss of her hearing, she took an overdose of sleeping pills on New Year's Day, 1960.

Hollywood Murders

Comedian Phil Hartman was shot to death by his wife. Character actor Victor Kilian was murdered by burglars who broke into his Hollywood apartment. Sad to say, everyone on this list was murdered.

1. SHARON TATE

Sharon Tate, a gorgeous actress who starred in *Valley of the Dolls* and *The Fearless Vampire Killers,* was married to director Roman Polanski. On August 8, 1969, the pregnant 26-year-old actress was murdered in her Cielo Drive home by members of the Manson family. Four of Tate's friends also were slain in the massacre.

2. BOB CRANE

Bob Crane starred in the popular television series *Hogan's Heroes* from 1965 to 1971. On June 29, 1978, the 49-year-old actor was bludgeoned to death in his apartment in Scottsdale, Arizona. During coverage of his murder, it was revealed that Crane was a sexual addict. Sixteen years later, John Henry Carpenter, an acquaintance of Crane, was tried for his murder, but was acquitted.

3. **DOROTHY STRATTEN**

Dorothy Stratten was a *Playboy* Playmate and one of the stars of *They All Laughed.* She fell in love with the film's director, Peter Bogdanovich. On August 14, 1980, the 20-year-old beauty was shotgunned to death by her estranged husband, Paul Snyder.

4. **RAMON NOVARRO**

Ramon Novarro played Ben-Hur in the 1926 silent version. The former silent film idol was murdered in his Hollywood Hills home. The 69-year-old actor was beaten brutally, and his killers reportedly rammed a black art deco dildo, a gift from Rudolph Valentino, down his throat. Two male hustlers, Paul and Tom Ferguson, were convicted of the crime.

5. **REBECCA SCHAEFFER**

Rebecca Schaeffer was a talented young actress, best known for her work on the television series *My Sister Sam.* On July 18, 1989, Schaeffer was scheduled to audition for a role in *The Godfather III.* That morning, she answered the door and was shot to death by 19-year-old Robert Bardo, a fan obsessed with her. Rebecca Schaeffer was only 20 years old.

6. **SAL MINEO**

Thirty-seven-year-old Sal Mineo was stabbed to death outside his West Hollywood apartment on February 13, 1976. Mineo had been nominated for Oscars for his performances in *Rebel Without a Cause* and *Exodus.* Two years later, a man named Lionel Williams was charged with his murder. Apparently, the killing had been a senseless random act of violence.

7. DOMINIQUE DUNNE

Twenty-three-year-old Dominique Dunne, who starred in the 1982 box office smash *Poltergeist,* was strangled in her West Hollywood apartment by her ex-boyfriend, John Sweeney. Near death, Dunne was rushed to the hospital where she was connected to a life-support machine. She died five days later, on November 4, 1982.

8. CARL SWITZER

Carl Switzer played Alfalfa in the *Our Gang* comedies. After he left the *Our Gang* series in 1941, his acting roles were few and far between. On January 29, 1959, the 31-year-old Switzer was shot to death in an argument over a hunting dog.

9. WILLIAM DESMOND TAYLOR

On February 1, 1922, director William Desmond Taylor was shot to death in the study of his Los Angeles apartment. The investigation revealed that Taylor was a notorious ladies' man. Two actresses romantically linked to him, Mabel Normand and Mary Miles Minter, saw their careers damaged irreparably by the scandal. The murder was never solved.

10. JUDITH BARSI

In 1984, seven-year-old Judith Barsi played a child murdered by her father in the made-for-television movie *Fatal Vision.* Four years later, Barsi actually was murdered by her father, Jozsef, who also killed his wife.

The Last Word

I n *Citizen Kane,* a reporter spends the entire movie trying to find out the meaning of Charles Foster Kane's last word, "Rosebud." Let's end the book with some of the last words said by Hollywood stars.

1. GEORGE SANDERS

Academy Award–winning actor George Sanders committed suicide in Spain on April 25, 1972. The 65-year-old washed down five vials of Nembutal with vodka. He left a suicide note that read: "Dear World: I am leaving because I am bored. I am leaving with your worries in this sweet cesspool. Good luck."

2. DOUGLAS FAIRBANKS

Douglas Fairbanks, one of the most popular stars of the silent film era, died on December 12, 1939, at the age of 56. His last words were, "I never felt better."

3. JOHN CARRADINE

Veteran actor John Carradine visited Milan, Italy, in 1982. Although he was 82 years old, Carradine insisted on climbing the 328 steps to the top of the cathedral. As he looked over the city, he said, "Milan—what a beautiful place to die!" Carradine collapsed and died three days later. At the funeral, his son, actor David Carradine, was unhappy with the grotesque smile molded on his father's face by the mortician. He poured half a bottle of scotch, his father's favorite drink, down John's throat and rearranged his expression to a more natural one.

4. JAMES DEAN

On September 30, 1955, James Dean died in an automobile accident at the intersection of routes 41 and 466 near Paso Robles, California. Seconds before impact, Dean turned to passenger Rolf Weutherich and said, "He's got to see us."

5. LOU COSTELLO

Comedian Lou Costello had a heart attack on February 26, 1959. Five days later, while Costello was recovering, he drank a strawberry ice cream soda. "That's the best ice cream soda I ever tasted," Costello said, and then died.

6. HUMPHREY BOGART

Humphrey Bogart lost his long battle with cancer on January 14, 1957. Apparently the illness didn't diminish Bogart's sense of humor. Reportedly, his last words were, "I never should have switched from scotch to martinis."

7. **W. C. FIELDS**

W. C. Fields died on Christmas Day, 1946. According to his mistress, Carlotta Monti, his last words were, "God damn the whole friggin' world and everybody in it but you, Carlotta."

8. **DICK SHAWN**

Dick Shawn was a comic actor best remembered for his performance in *It's a Mad, Mad, Mad, Mad World* and *The Producers.* Shawn loved to perform in front of a live audience. On April 18, 1987, the 63-year-old comedian was appearing at the University of California in San Diego. He was performing a routine about the end of the world when he said, "And I would be your leader." Shawn collapsed, and everyone in the audience thought it was part of the bit. Shawn lay there for minutes while the audience laughed. Finally, a doctor rushed to his aid, but Shawn was pronounced dead of cardiac arrest shortly after arriving at the hospital.

9. **NELSON EDDY**

Nelson Eddy and Jeanette MacDonald appeared in eight musicals together between 1935 and 1942. When MacDonald died in 1965, Eddy sang their signature song, "Ah, Sweet Mystery of Life," at her funeral. On March 6, 1967, Eddy was performing at the Blue Sails Room in Miami Beach, Florida, when he told an interviewer, "I'm working harder than I ever have in my life...I hope to keep going until I drop." That evening he was performing a song when he suddenly stopped. He apologized to the audience, saying, "Will you bear with me a minute? I can't seem to get the words out." After a moment of struggling to remember the words he exclaimed, "I can't see! I can't hear!" and collapsed. Eddy had suffered a stroke and passed away the next day.

10. **MEL BLANC**

Mel Blanc provided the voices for most of the Looney Tunes characters: Bugs Bunny, Daffy Duck, Porky Pig, Tweety, Sylvester, Yosemite Sam, Foghorn Leghorn, and many others. When he died at age 81 on July 10, 1989, Blanc had instructed that the words "That's all folks!" be inscribed on his tombstone.

Bibliography

Amende, Coral. *Hollywood Confidential.* New York: Plume, 1997.

Anger, Kenneth. *Hollywood Babylon.* New York: Dell Publishing, 1981.

——. *Hollywood Babylon II.* New York: Plume, 1984.

Bartel, Pauline. *Amazing Animal Actors.* Dallas: Taylor Publishing, 1997.

Bernard, Jami. *First Films.* New York: Citadel Press, 1993.

Boller, Paul, Jr. *Hollywood Anecdotes.* New York: William Morrow & Co., 1987.

Brown, Gene. *Movie Time.* New York: Macmillan, 1995.

Callistro, Paddy, and Fred Basten. *The Hollywood Archive.* New York: Angel City Press, 2000.

Cawthorne, Nigel. *Sex Lives of the Hollywood Goddesses.* London: Prion Books, 2000.

Cini, Zelda, and Bob Crane. *Hollywood: Land and Legend.* Westport, Conn.: Arlington House, 1980.

Essoe, Gabe. *The Book of Movie Lists.* Westport, Conn.: Arlington House, 1981.

Feinman, Jeffrey. *Hollywood Confidential.* Chicago: Playboy Press, 1976.

Forbes, Malcolm. *They Went That-a-Way.* New York: Ballantine Books, 1988.

Givens, Bill. *Film Flubs.* New York: Citadel Press, 1990.

———. *Son of Film Flubs.* New York: Citadel Press, 1991.

Grey, Rudolph. *Nightmare of Ecstasy.* Los Angeles: Feral House, 1992.

Hadleigh, Boze. *Hollywood and Whine.* Secaucus, N.J.: Birch Lane Press, 1998.

Hansen-Steiger, Sherry, and Brad Steiger. *Hollywood and the Supernatural.* New York: St. Martin's Press, 1990.

Haun, Harry. *A Cinematic Century.* New York: Applause Books, 2000.

Lucaire, Ed. *The Celebrity Almanac.* New York: Prentice Hall, 1991.

Luijters, Guus, and Gerard Timmer. *Sexbomb.* Secaucus, N.J.: Citadel Press, 1988.

Malone, Aubrey. *I Was a Fugitive from a Hollywood Trivia Factory.* Chicago: Contemporary Books, 2000.

Martin, Mart. *Did He or Didn't He?* New York: Citadel Press, 2000.

———. *Did She or Didn't She?* New York: Citadel Press, 1996.

McCarty, John. *The Sleaze Merchants.* New York: St. Martin's Press, 1995.

Medved, Harry, and Michael Medved. *The Golden Turkey Awards.* New York: Berkley Books, 1980.

——. *Son of Golden Turkey Awards.* New York: Villard, 1986.

Nash, Bruce, and Allan Zullo. *The Hollywood Walk of Shame.* Kansas City: Andrews and McMeel, 1993.

Nash, Jay Robert. *Zanies.* Piscataway, N.J.: New Century Publishers, 1982.

Parish, James Robert. *The Hollywood Death Book.* Las Vegas: Pioneer Books, 1992.

Quinlan, David. *Quinlan's Film Stars.* Washington: Brassey's, 2000.

Robertson, Patrick. *The Guinness Book of Almost Everything You Didn't Need to Know about the Movies.* Enfield, U.K.: Guinness Books, 1986.

——. *The Guinness Book of Movie Facts and Feats.* New York: Abbeville Press, 1994.

Roeper, Richard. *Hollywood Urban Legends.* Franklin Lakes, N.J.: New Page Books, 2001.

Sealy, Shirley. *The Celebrity Sex Register.* New York: Fireside Books, 1982.

Sennett, Robert. *Hollywood Hoopla.* New York: Billboard Books, 1998.

Shipman, David. *Movie Talk.* New York: St. Martin's Press, 1988.

Sinclair, Marianne. *Hollywood Lolitas.* New York: Henry Holt & Co., 1988.

Sullivan, George. *Quotable Hollywood.* New York: Barnes & Noble, 2001.

Sullivan, Steve. *Glamour Girls.* New York: St. Martin's Press, 1999.

Van Daalen, Nicholas. *The Complete Book of Movie Lists.* Toronto: Pagurian Press, 1979.

Wallace, Irving, Amy Wallace, David Wallechinsky, and Sylvia Wallace. *The Intimate Sex Lives of Famous People.* New York: Delacorte Press, 1981.

Wallechinsky, David, Irving Wallace, and Amy Wallace. *The Book of Lists.* New York: William Morrow & Co., 1977.

Wiley, Mason, and Damien Bona. *Inside Oscar.* New York: Ballantine Books, 1993.

Wilkerson, Tichi, and Marcia Borie. *The Hollywood Reporter.* New York: Coward-McCann, 1984.

Index

About the Author

Floyd Conner is the author of biographies of film stars Tuesday Weld and Lupe Velez as well as *Baseball's Most Wanted, Golf's Most Wanted, Basketball's Most Wanted, The Olympics' Most Wanted, Football's Most Wanted, Wrestling's Most Wanted,* and *Tennis's Most Wanted.* He lives in Cincinnati, Ohio.